HONORABLE AMEND

75

Other Books by Michael S. Harper

Poetry

Dear John, Dear Coltrane
History Is Your Own Heartbeat
History as Appletree
Song: I Want a Witness
Debridement
Nightmare Begins Responsibility
Images of Kin: Selected Poems
Healing Song for the Inner Ear

Anthologies

Heartblow: Black Veils
Chant of Saints (co-editor)
Every Shut-Eye Ain't Asleep (co-editor)

HONORABLE AMENDMENTS

Poems by Michael S. Harper

University of Illinois Press   Urbana and Chicago

Publication of this book was supported by a grant from
the Illinois Arts Council, a state agency.

© 1995 by Michael S. Harper
Manufactured in the United States of America
1 2 3 4 5 C P 5 4 3 2 1

This book is printed on acid-free paper.

Library of Congress Cataloging-in-Publication Data

Harper, Michael S., 1938–
    Honorable amendments : poems / by Michael S. Harper.
        p.   cm.
    ISBN 0-252-02143-6 (cloth : alk. paper). — ISBN 0-252-06514-X
(paper : alk. paper)
    I. Title.
PS3558.A6248H66   1995
811'.54—dc20   95-17098
                                                                        CIP

For my father, W. Warren Harper

We grew up in an age when one conveyed thoughts to one another by letter, and they were read over and over. Letters have been a great source in gathering material about family, even a few things that were kept secret. Ours was the age of children who were meant to be seen and not heard. Katherine must have been one of the great eavesdroppers, she knew so many priceless details. So I will write letters to our children, parents, relatives, and my wife. I will refer to her as Katherine, Kate (her grandmother's name), Katti, a family name, Babe, my pet name—after all I grew up in the Babe Ruth era and to be called Babe meant you were the greatest. Katherine, our daughter, is named after her mother, so she is always Kath to us.

We have lived through four wars, three while married, the Great Depression, Prohibition, the rise of organized crime, and the labor union strife, to name only a few. So I will supplement the story with events or incidents, both personal and general.

I am including a genealogy: this can be used to establish a Harper/Johnson lineage.

Most of Katti's Brooklyn life revolved around 902 Lafayette Ave.

When we moved to Los Angeles we lived at 2207 So. Orange Drive so our life now revolved around this home. We were not much on moving about. Katti always said she didn't want to move from Orange Drive, because the present generations did lots of moving, but all of our grandchildren, who spent time here, will know that we are still where they first met us. This is home.

—From *I'm Katherine: A Memoir,*
by W. Warren Harper

I don't know why my mother wants to stay here fuh
This ol' world ain't been no friend to huh
    —traditional

It's a wise blues that knows its father
    —traditional

I been down so long that down don't worry me
    —traditional

"The Arkansas Traveler"
—A painting by Edward Payson Washburn
—An American strategy of humor in which Americans face their critics by pretending to be even dumber than they are expected to be, all the while undercutting their opponents by a play of witty double entendre. (The classic encounter is between a farmer and a city slicker, but a close look at the opposing values reveals that the antagonists symbolize the New World and the Old.)

Representatives and direct Taxes shall be apportioned among the several States which may be included within the Union, according to their respective Numbers, which shall be determined by adding to the whole Number of free Persons, including those bound to Service for a Term of Years, and excluding Indians not taxed, *three fifths of all other Persons.*

> —The Constitution of the United
> States, art. 1, sec. 2(3)
> (proposed in 1787, ratified in 1789)

By a "commitment to democracy" I mean a commitment to the idea that there are no fixed or determinable limits to the capacities of any individual human being, and that all are entitled, by inalienable right, to equal opportunities to develop their potentialities. Democracy in this sense is an ideal, not a political system, and certainly not an actual state of affairs.

> —*The Beer Can by the Highway,*
> by John A. Kouewenhoven

Contents

Acknowledgments

The following poems first appeared in these journals:

Antaeus: "Josh Gibson's Bat"; "Lecturing on a Theme of Motherhood"; "My Students Who Stand in Snow"

Black Warrior Review: "Ulysses S. Grant: His Prose"; "It Is the Man/Woman Outside Who Judges"; "The Line: How to Step Out of It"; "Intentional Suffering"; "Changing Names in the Streets"

Brown Alumni Monthly: "The Revolutionary Garden"

Brown University Library Journal: "Mr. Knowlton Predicts"

Caliban: "Studs"; "Portrait of James Weldon Johnson"; "Pardons (from A. Lincoln)"; "Free Associations: Some Practical Symbols"

Callaloo: "Angola (Louisiana)"; "Dexter Leaps In"; "Saint Sassy Divine"; "The Sanctity of the Unwritten"; "My Father at 75"; "Songlines from a Tessera(e) Journal"; "Fanny's Kitchen"; "Teaching Institutes"; "Hinton's Silkscreens"

Clerestory: "Parenting"; "Thimble"

Contemporary American Poetry: "Protégé: 1962"

Crazyhorse: "The Ghost of Soul-making"; "Changes on Coleman 'Bean' Hawkins's Birthday"; "Mule"

Cutbank: "Manong: Angola"

Graham House Review: "Jest: A Collection of Records"; "Late September Refrain"

Gulf Coast: "The Beauty Shell"; "'Dixie Peach'"; "Fixit"

The Kenyon Review: "Prologue of an Arkansas Traveler"

The New Republic: "To an Old Old Man Twiddlin' Thumbs"

Princeton Library Journal: "My Father's Face"

Providence Sunday Journal: "Rhode Island (SSBNT740): A Toast"

TriQuarterly: "Study Windows"

The Washington Post: "Advice to Clinton"

ONE

~

A Po' Man's Heart Disease

Ulysses S. Grant: His Prose

With Twain's check and the clock stopped,
the nation thought of uniforms, Lee's white
suit, emblazoned sword, the best of cabin.

Stuck up on a horse, Grant lacked ambition,
went out in the cold at Shiloh
so the surgeons could operate in peace;
hated greenbacks, perhaps encouraged baseball
by refusing annexation of Santo Domingo.

Discovered, in his own blood, at Palo Alto,
the cause of the war; his favorite chair,
small, even for his 5'7" frame, he wrapped
his bad throat in confluence, morphine and cocaine,
two rivers at Paducah, the "slow cottage" razor blade
fence of the mountaintop, which he'd seen over.

"Hiram," his brand of whiskey, was only his name;
out over the Hudson he was never seasick,
the waves a tablecloth, notes in his saddlebag;
in weaponry, money, the fate of numbers,
he hid his wit in fairness, ran from the presidency,
scout's honor, turned his back on "The Crater."

He preferred robust Mt. McGregor, overlooking the lake
where no traitor could come, save in medium halter;
fair, without romance, the 15th Amendment under belt,
he took God's punishment (south of the border)
into his memoirs, having seized the Ohio River,
a drinker's disease of vernacular stories,
into hapless slaughter, shining blank pages.

It Is the Man/Woman Outside Who Judges

PART 1

"Intimacy of speech, is history, made art."

"The blues ain't nothin'
but a po' man's disease"
is what he thought
in Jan Smuts Airport:
he was carrying books,
poetry, with black people
on the cover—his Afrikaans
was terrible, being from Brooklyn,
wintering in L.A.;
at Iowa, the river
was shallow except in spring;
artists, driven to madness
by deadlines and grades,
often jumped, forgot to duck,
worked with the current
to the banks, where somebody
without a rowboat or an oar
gave a hand,
didn't report you.
You went home to paint,
sculpt, write your sonnet;
the world of Robert Frost
and Lowell, Amy and Robert,
was running again,

if you could swim:
this was before aerobic flight,
overdrive, running marathons
in the barracks workshop—
this was the time of *Jubilee,*
the whole Civil War on acetate;
one trope from Miriam Makeba
all you needed for orals,
for thesis on Yeats
and *Invisible Man,*
not to speak of Emily,
who spoke to no one
on most days, lexicon
for modernism, morality
play of words, gestures,
fatherhood, the wrong mentors.

Dakar and Goree
the poet-president
raising money in Paris,
Banjul the first stop
to Juffure,
Roots in *Newsweek,*
the griot just recently dead.
Ghana and *ananse* in Accra,
the drive to Cape Coast,
Elmina and Kumasi,
your poet-friend saying good-bye
forever when he saw blood
on the ceiling, saw his own blood
turn inward to the spacious hymn,
saved by Anglican dogma, ICA light.

To dine at castle in Kumasi,
the robes of Asantehene,
the silver tray, the golden stool;
Lagos, sealed in the airport
cabin, served by Ethiopians
about to defect;

the Kinshasa airport,
Lumumba's last good-bye—
Ralph Bunche's specter long gone.

On ETA some French wine
on a planeload of Afrikaners
fresh from Nice,
refusing your baggage,
your lost cool, the power of wings
soothed by the French stewardess,
your spotty French better
than vernacular Dutch,
cadences of Dutch elm disease
on American tree-lined streets;
on the tail of Andrew Young,
his tears at Azanian brothers,
their rush for suits,
police uniforms, packed somites
in commuter trains to the city
of gold, diamonds, studs

PART 2

Tongues, that making of vowels
over land, the land broken
in syntax, syntactical slavery:
charting of bloodlines,
caretaker of tongues.

T.J. on horseback
at river crossings:
he cannot cross over
easily, true patriot,
pacifist in the bedroom,
the free black community,
sacred ballast for engineers,
wiped clean in arcs of progress,
the great agrarian way.

In white sails and white coats
the Pullman cars come into view;
all the leather initials,
every linen cabinet in daybook
travel, end in the washroom:

"the *nigger* is living proof
that Indians fucked buffalo."

She stands at the crossroads
of the Natchez Trace,
half-breed Sacagawea,
mother of Big Harpe,
sister of Little Harpe,
waving the lanterns
to three heads posted
on a sour-apple tree.

The octoroons of Carter Braxton's
hamlet surely visualized the Niger:
with cannons trained on sphinx,
in Haitian waters,

on the Alhambra;
the Sufis walk in kente cloth.

The reed cries out in separate
unction, amending sacred names:

Mr. Jefferson walks the territory
of his original purchase,
all the land that Coltrane needs to play.

The Line: How to Step Out of It

A boy can now stand tall,
the Klan, on foot or in cars,
stand in the womb.

In the courthouse
he fixes the teeth
of a wayward cross.

The pitcher's mound, outside Roanoke, in twilight:
the count, 3 & 2 in the ninth inning,
hovers like a starling at the perfect game.

Just then, already wound up, he glimpses the 1233
coming up the rise—calls time—walks to the fence.
His wave to the fireman is a Masonic wave—back on the mound.

The shadow of a gondola crosses the magic circle;
he could be accused of grease, being a doctor of the fast-
ball; he could doctor all the stitching in Haiti.

He couldn't cheat for the best batter in the world,
Josh Gibson, framed on his haunches, at Yankee Stadium.
The good dentist has testified for jury review.

He has squired the four freed Scottsboro boys
out of town in his roadster; he strikes out Josh
without touching the bill of his cap.

The game is almost over; the body, at half-rest
in the words of the sacred pyre, is ash in the blaze
of a Sunday afternoon. Dream merchant of the perfect game.

"Dr. Frank J. Sykes," you have lived your frolic
in our memories of you, and in our book of names.

Intentional Suffering

The hat turned to match the trimmed mustache;
the basepaths you trod at Morehouse in white bucks;
the whole world on newsreel riding taxis called
"Free Ride to Heaven" and *Hate* Bus—
Kennedy, on new wheels, and partial to Hollywood,
comes to the rescue, with troops; recruits,
with upturned helmets, pray for early leave.

One horse, dead on arrival at Cottonwood,
is put to death again on the operating table,
the thrashing of his shattered stump
spraying the ceiling, smocks, doorhandles.
This is a horse that belongs to the mounted police.

The king of Sweden watched agog; on the elevator
in the old section of Stockholm *An America Dilemma*
becomes the practical light in the storm—
the scholars of the thirties put it down for good.

Eavesdropping by electrodes comes to your door;
your children wake up and sleep quiet
to choir flashbacks to Genesis, the Golden Rule.
You finger the cotton robes given at gravesites;
you think of Sam Hose and Bennie Mays—
you promise anything to the country's conscience
in a hotel lobby, for cameras, for NPR.

Boston looks better the closer you get to the mountain-
top, which isn't Memphis or Birmingham, but Oslo,
when you were almost free from the FBI.

Ida, the housemaid from Augusta, Georgia,
walks to work on the day of your death
in a pink smock which she refuses to change.

Her son works at the arsenal; he moves furniture
for the good people of the military base
with an impish smile: his prayers are daily
prayers; on Sundays he gardens his own patch.

He remembers his mother's first impressions
of the good white people of the South,
with their lights on,
while the debate goes on for peace;
the family does not know his mother's surname.
He makes sure nothing shifts in the half-ton
that will scar or break on the turns
going by the military base. His text,
written in his mother's blood, is in capital letters.

Changing Names in the Streets

*"Be ashamed to die until you have won some victory
for humanity."*
        —Martin Luther King, Jr.

You look over the map for directions;
only a few years back everybody went
to different schools; on River Road
you can pass under two trestles, one
highway going to Mississippi.
My daughter wants to know everything
about Stevie Wonder's campaign
for your national holiday—
she wants to take off on your music,
the art of the flesh of your voice,
without going to any church in the land,
wants to turn on the radio, tune in on FM,
hates the grass of public outings
because of chiggers in the grass—
there are no bulletproof blankets
in a spinach field, no matter how
many shacks are planted.

The map is without your name
though you can drive into the country
without any traffic lights;
the black kids, at 20 mph,
dart into a Shell station for gas,
take off for the game,
under the lights this evening.

You remember the Watts riot, 1965:
from the high tower of glass
minorities, with jobs, heard
the whine of the helicopters
as if for the first time—
they were late for work, or early
in the swing shift, and the National
Guard was neutral—the police were not.

Truck farmers got their headlights broken
for stopping at roadblocks;
kids shot across the freeways;
the comfort stations of clean mt. dew
are in the dry riverbed.

We have prayed for rain in Washington;
we have rubbed the mixed messages
of our neighbors, our own attitudes,
the color schemes of housing
where we sell out all.

How to live in a circle, just off-campus,
the parking lot filled with tailgaters
to the hum of "Roll Tide."

I have been on your boulevard
through the black neighborhoods,
upside down, looking for ribs, tasting compost.

Free Associations: Some Practical Symbols

Jitneys: soundings like chitterlings
but the machine is Mercedes Benz;
why did you put them together
like you tore them apart,
Watusi taxi-man in dreadlocks,
the aneurysm hidden in rattling
bones along the wisdom craters:
skull and crossbones of cherished curlicues.

For Malcolm: pick of the litter;
German shepherds, huge and pleasant,
are rare; in the East Palo Alto
neighborhood he was mythic,
his 5' white mistress
on her leash of commitments
at the post office,
while you went to school
down on the farm.
On campus you lived as king
of electrodes,
rebuilding motors
to the rainbow computers
where your children could eat
to the tune of "Giant Steps."

Suddenly dysplasia in the lair,
the brain as bleeding faucet,
as hip disease,
the neighbors, on blues changes,
into reggae, into TV.

Lacquer: housepaint's bad for nails,
but your long strokes made glitter
of walls and ceilings
come alive in forearms,
hinges of the workgang's dance;
you wrote in rhymes in rags
to semiliterate housegangs,
the light enamel of your fingers
the lost bids of your woman aflame,
the need for children,
Italy transplanted,
enough to make you the pasta-man you were,
shogun of the dynasty,
the black patrone.

Freeway [Contra Costa College]
Approach: Semiotics on the road
from the projects, the shipyards,
doped corridors of fog to Tahoe,
your text the panthers in Sacramento;
when you black out on prednisone
or digitalis
the wagon of mercy
picks you up in the back seat
of your jitney

                    off the freeway,
your library books and rollsheet
scattered in the breakdown lane,
sagas you couldn't write without octane,
body fluids for the brain stations,
the soft programs of revolution.

Watts Riot: born to conventional parents
where race meant little,
next to the little tower of pisa
made of glass
you couldn't paint in your sleep,
schooled on Mingus,
the same height as Dexter Gordon,

down the street of dream merchants,
having learned to play:
what did you need with matches,
the blowtorch of your mind
alive in strings of pearls,
rushing your story
of dialysis,
the kidney shutdown of friends,
vagrant hole-in-the-wall gardens
for America on television,
the mustard gas of the 60's.

    Shipyard: Mays astride the fence in center
the whole decade,
watching the flag through gales of fog,
freezing in the bleachers,
the famed side-ache of #24
sambo doll hitting into the teeth
of Candlestick,
the flattop of your experience
with weapons,
out on bad discharge papers.

Later, after talking back to the brass,
you jammed on sonar, Dorie Miller's story
in iambic pentameter,
and Miles Davis asleep on Singapore slings.

The poor of every race forgot the U.N.
on VJ Day, strolled in the park,
fixed Volkswagons, opened camps
begun at Santa Anita,
hamlets of Agent Orange
on the lost grace notes of blue and green.

    Cranial Cap: All the innards outside
to patch the aneurysm—you were like new,
the gears above the neck
alive in blackouts,
running off the road,

where you could not eat,
the greasy spoons of friends
broken on your attention span;
the spread of flatpaint
no enamel—there were no offspring—
developed asthma—
breathed pure oxygen of the valley
on utility jobs—
became the heavy hitter of the veld,
doped up on smog and steroids:
to gut the skull to stop the bleeding;
to teach the lessons of the body
decomposing on the throne,
to laugh as the throne sits empty,
without pharaoh's spirit,
the life of the tomb,
in kingship time
a wilderness, aloneness:
the cap of the skull is clean.

—*In memory of James V. Blake*

Study Windows

The two Germans,
both in their seventies,
were Americans
only by birth;
for $2.50/hour
they put up
a fourteen-foot-
square study,
oak paneling,
four windows
three feet square
to see the sun,
feel the lake,
touch the trees.

These men said
"they were worthless,"
had lost their zing
in their fifties,
chased women only
in springtime,
forgot the chase
of the bottle
save for Christmas.

The older one died
on the ladder
of another job,
laughing to putterings
of his heart muscle,
which gave out
on too much benzine,

bright colorations
of cured wood,
the handle of the womb
he touched as a boy,
as a man learned to wash
with the schnapps of semen
he said his father
brought from the old country.

You code your life
with the ability to work,
work at that
even while fishing;
only on the hunt
do you lie down,
the red gear
the antlers of the view
a square window.

Smooth ice, a dusting
of snow; for this world
tracks, the ruddered imprint,
the hammering of nails
so one can see.

Late September Refrain

"A love supreme."

Years have gone by without a single
ceremony to your name; the tunes,
greater in scale than the mountains,
stand and shine. Out of the darkness,
the hardest objective of the light,
come your arpeggios,
a way of saying water
running uphill
at great speed.

In Mexico the bodies of our soldiers,
our sisters and brothers,
are found under pick and shovel;
the dogs, flown in from America,
which is our country,
and our continent,
find our survivors.

I was there in the depths of the museums,
with the children on holiday
in the central park,
the park without pesos and tourists,
on the day you died.

Now I hear the tributes come from Boston
a week in advance,
and I hear the music of today.

In Bombay, next to the Taj Mahal,
I heard the sitar of Ravi Shankar
bring in the dawn,

and the islands off Elephanta
bring in the fishes.

I saw you pray, over coffee,
and vexed to cry over your instrument,
and your fast car, the station
wagon, going uptown to hear Bud
Powell, just after his return home.

Today's your birthday;
I expect little, having been blessed,
countless times,
by your reed and mouthpiece.
A mouthpiece is different from a reed,
which flanges into the spaces of the mouth
where even spit evaporates to the song.

The mouthpiece is the tunnel,
viaduct, headband of the sun;
it is the fields, and the call of the fields.
It is shining in your example:
I say your name: John William Coltrane.
I say the refrain: *a love supreme!*

—*For John S. Wright*

Arthritis Dance

Downwind from the Havana
he's chewed through the butt
he thinks about mortician science,
a mailhandler's bag
he learned to swing on the route—
routes south and west to Omaha—
meat-packing country, where the Globe-
trotters came to picnic at the platform.

In his Dodger cap he muses over
Robinson, Campanella,
the boy-Mays capturing his twin cities;
for a share of the gate,
brought back from retirement,
he puts his brown hands
on the gate to the orchard: how he sprayed
apples so the worm wouldn't camp
at the core.

Kids next door threw apples in Indian
wars, and his kids, kept in from riffraff,
integrated the schools. The old homestead
had bushels of apples, killed all the taste
his children had for seeds of paradise;
still he misses the blossoms, the bees,
bats that invade any house with rafters,
where you hang your hall-of-fame posters
to discrimination, the race's music,
so you beef yourself up on coaching,
take the cod-liver oil to ease the spine
rusting with age, come loose
over satchels and yard chores,

tunes of women lifted to the bedstead
where Little Crow crowed before battle
and the sacred bones disappeared
as toothaches, applecores, panetellas.

—*For Boyd Wright*

To an Old Man Twiddlin' Thumbs

You sit twiddlin' thumbs
"beat out," watching
your wife watch you watch her:
all this watching twiddlin' thumbs.

My children fidget while you balance
thumb controls on local news,
excerpts from a recent book on slavery,
and we finally have the scale of twiddlin' thumbs.

Old man, remember the chemistry
for your depression is alchemical.
I set out my convivial tools
measuring your need, measuring your index
finger, your thumbnails, your wife
"beat out" in her slavery of affection
for your genius at disguise.

Old man, my pestle works for your recovery;
old man, the conjure knowledge is "beat out"
with alkaline and tea,
this nightmare where you've lost your way home:
old man, the strong men must come on.

Angola (Louisiana)

Three-fourths Mississippi
River, one-fourth rattlesnakes,
and for company, razorwire
fences, experiments from South
Africa, aging behind bars,
all in their seventies,
with no parole; perhaps
2500 natural life sentences,
30-year lifers behind bars.

Still, the roads have flowers;
and in the prison hospital
the Lifers Association creed
is in full bloom, technical
supernovas of the TV world:
you avoid mirrors as you can't
avoid hard labor, false teeth,
high blood pressure, rape:
all this in the prison magazine.

Wheelchair has transcended mirrors;
he dreams about theft and harassment
as a prison underwater,
decompression channels of the bends,
cheap guards in scuba tanks,
for he is never coming up;
it is "too exotic," he says,
and you hunger for the fields
you were broken in;
you hunger for your white neighbors,
dragon deputies, the KKK,

as you count the gray hairs
on the sideview of your mustache.

After three heart attacks
you can stand gospel music,
sports, violence, drugs,
for deathrow education
is bimonthly books,
the old folks' home on this shuttle.

I was born on False River:
tell my story in amplitude
from one slavery to another;
give me the pure medicine
for rape, murder, the nectar
in balm for the barroom fight:
teach me to read, and write.

—*For Ernest J. Gaines*

TWO

~

Songlines from a Tessera(e) Journal

But had you accepted him as an incarnation of Sambo, you would have missed a very courageous man—a man who understood only too well that his activities in aiding and protecting the young Northern students working in the Freedom Movement placed his life in constant contact with death, but continued to act. Now, I'm not going to reject that man because some misinformed person, some prejudiced person, sees him as the embodiment of Uncle Tom or Sambo. What's inside you, brother; what's your heart like? What are your real values? What human qualities are hidden beneath your idiom?

—Ralph Waldo Ellison

Songlines from a Tessera(e) Journal: Romare Bearden, 1912–88

"A style is achieved by an artist through his introduction of personal forms into the grand style of his period."

QUILTING BEE (MECKLENBURG COUNTY)

"Re PLUMMER ALEXANDER, born in August 1853,
in North Carolina near Charlotte, near the porch
which he leapt from to travel north with Union
soldiers, Sherman's returning army, in 1865.
He was sitting on a fence, which was kin to the porch,
when troops passed by; one soldier offered to take
him north—Plummer never said good-bye.
                              When he got to New York
worked his way to the stature of Huntington Harford's
valet; had been a "runner" on Wall Street; was taught to
read (as an adult) by his wife, Francis Moore, whom he met
          in Ithaca.*
What a resonant, mellifluous voice; returned home
to buy shoes for his mother; always reserved a Pullman
to avoid segregated travel. Loved trains; had trouble
with that mode of travel. Lived in East New York
into his eighties, walking miles to work in weather.
Any information you might find in state records
most appreciated."
                              This over the bunting:
the diamonds and gold of musicians humming without
          voice.

*Underground railroad station (N.Y.)

31

HOMAGE TO THE BROWN BOMBER

Speed of the punch,
its dancing, rhythmic fluency
in short space, short duration,
its honing light of the Garden,
the Stadium: each gladiator falls
to be redeemed in porcelain speech,
however simple, never glib,
the nation's devastation
coming home to roost.

Born near sacred Indian mounds in Alabama,
broken in the "destroy" kitchens
of Chevrolet and Cadillac,
short tours at Comiskey Park,
the heavy bag the strange fruit
of commerce, newsprint,
without the dazzling photographs
of Sonja Henie's pirouettes
at the Olympic Games,
in shared bedrooms, horns
plenty for the unprotected.

Sugar dazzled too,
but the brute poetry
of the finisher,
how to wait on hidden impulse
of a bannered song,
that was ammunition
for the lost struggle
of the chaingang,
of the limousine.

Taps at Vegas,
new shrubbery
at Arlington,
grist for radio, the stooped flares
of camels

on deserts of yesterdays,
bright lungs blanching tomorrows,
barrows at rest.

JOURNEY THROUGH THE INTERIOR

*"There is unfortunately no bridge between the fine arts
and the arts of commerce. The artist must decide which
of the two endeavors is most compatible to his talents
and personality. . . ."*

the unity is actual placement of stones
    its purpose: enhancement without disturbance

closure, its rests, grids, agitated surfaces
    bars of music, vertical control

I entered my canvas in Masonic calm,
    the open corner, with natural linen
    as all baptism is tearing upward
    astride flat surfaces
    with immaculate rice paper
scale is always the cut-out
    lost silhouettes:

    "it was like looking at pretty girls
and not being able to see beautiful women"

    It was strenuous repetition
    tempering of volumes
    as keys on Earl Hines's righteous
    black keys, its tensions
    overlapping the planes,
    the music of optics.

One avoids defeat when judgment comes slowly,
    mysterious as creation itself:
    structure often appears far apart
from images that animate dreams—
    no matter the effects they launch
are representational or decorative in nature.

    Nymphs at infinite depth,
    the bird is the fish the soldier the dancer:
    he who plays the inner music;
    she, the word, in aquarium.

ODD FACTS ABOUT THE PAINTER (ON CAUSALITY)

"A realized structure is exacting in its spiritual and intellectual demands, and it unites such complexities as a sense of the past, as well as the total response of the painter to his craft, to himself, and to the life about him."

because robust sense of humor
    more subtle than tunes
    played in the head
    full of books, handkerchiefs,
    appurtenances at shared studios;
because conversations mean dance,
    vital steps for musicians
              who walk on their horns,
    their reedy tongues praise-gossip
because Savoy had good stride-piano
    tusks of Arabian cloth / Hannibal's elephant nights
because we cut this crazy quilt for Aïda,
    paste up for Judith Jamison,
    sketch cranial wall of Negro
    History Week, crater cave drawings
    most subtle, opaque modern cube of subway;

because a few spatial conventions
    (slavery, transatlantic triangular
    trade, econometric wood carvings,
    aesthetics of man, color combinations—
    mestizos / olé orishas—pictorial errors,
    miscegenated dross: the gene pool:)

because various problems of relationship
    condense negative space of temperament

why "Blue & Sentimental"
why "Jubilee Singers"
    why no bitterness in warm travels
    from Yoruba village to the block
    why block stays empty
    why roulette wheel to vespers

why accented songbirds in large spaces
why ecstasy, why agony
because confidence is hand-papered
paintings at joists, hoeing
vertical connective tissue,
circles of transition,
children of Circé

because victory garden
   why report of munition
because unseen armature of soul
   why spirit faces in masks
   of breastbone, leg irons,
   leg bones, legba ginny
   because welfare avocation
   turns umbrella inside out
   because convex/concave tropes
   why primitive influence (man as art form)
   more expressive than technical
because nature worship means end of nature
   why Fang figure
   because meteors fallen on alien landscape
   (blacks in the South)
   why they belong there
   always cubicle projection:
   ritual love: the other monotheism: radius lens.

Thanks for the drawing of Judith Jamison.
Thanks for the color separation of six
Odysseus collages, a portion of the sequence
in ritual brightness; thanks for the suggestions
of Hannibal as a tactician; thanks for educating
William Carlos Williams about the pictorial phrase.
Thanks for having your own donated pictures framed
at your own expense at the Hilton Hotel (N.Y.C.)
for the Black Academy of Arts & Letters—
standing in line for the shrimp cocktail
was a ritual experience—one could hear the music
of Chick Webb and Lester Young at the Savoy
because you put it there in your rock formations,
contests better, at the level of art, than the Apollo,
no bad feat in bear markets. Thanks for all your visual
puns, blind alleys, pig Latin collage: what you said
about Picasso: "the artist's sense of space is something
at which he gradually arrives, and then usually keeps
intact the rest of his life." Thanks for making the calluses,
that knowledge that soaks through to your hands; thanks
for wanting to do so. Thanks for the opening:
how to get to the unseen, how to get off welfare,
roadmaps of the G.I. Bill, World War II,
discrimination, preaching, rent control,
rent parties, Masonic orders, April in Paris.
Thanks for first steps etched to radio,
your own imitations hidden in the dark;
thanks for the pictorial limp, in sacred territory,
of the gangs; thanks for the strawboss calling our names;
thanks for the secret society of a man and a woman
reclining, standing tall, shopping at the early market,
drinking at the late; thanks for the waltz of Ladies
Night, Blue Monday, "kitchen mechanics," the Harlem curfew,
the bouncers that control clubs, fair fights with ground rules;
thanks for the gang rules, marathons, jitterbug reputations;
thanks for not getting caught in "Movietone News"; thanks

for "having a ball doing whatever came into my head" through
those knowledgeable hands; thanks for reading Delacroix's
        journal;
thanks for listening to Claude McKay; thanks for not being
        thrown
by "air steps," thanks for your own brand of eavesdropping,
making it an architonic experience which speaks volumes;
thanks for that elite demographics, going downtown to museums
and uptown to museums, and, as Lester Young used to do:
"catch the rhythm of the dancers which always comes back to you
when you're playing." Thanks for your pace at the fair.

THREE

~

Saint Sassy Divine

Impertinent Correspondence

*"How shall the mind keep warm save at the spectral
fires—how thrive but by the light of paradox?"*
   —"Stars," by Robert Hayden

"Bodily decrepitude is wisdom."
   —William Butler Yeats

As your publisher, in limited
edition, we must go to press,
so the eyeball you see as naked
aggression is only the world,
though we can feel your reach
in quasars, religious faith,
immunizes against our wish
to die, how we treat the child
alive in the man,
but only barely,
and not in this time zone:
(paradise valley)
logometric seizures of the bends.

In praxis,
padre of the coordinating conjunctions,
lowest of the low
to spirituals on the rooftops,
Lincoln comes to the rest
on the Natchez Trace,
Indian path through wilderness,
meadow and river
a forest fire shaman,
weathervanes over the centuries,
when we can barely count.

Senator Brooke called
about your passport,
which is hard to do
without a birth certificate,
but having to read to the Senate
by invitation,
art supersedes politics:
even the Eskimos
in their unlettered song-
poems
store up heat in glaciers
where Henson
spoke in immaculate tongue;
and he had children:

we end up in parlance,
on a shield, peacock,
outsider at odd angles,
leaping at the endstop
of the pit:
    I accept *His* grace.

Portrait of James Weldon Johnson

Atlanta Archives

The rolled cigar: Nicaragua politics,
the jazz age sequestered 'round midnight;
NAACP business around the clock.

His novel a mystery,
certainly "autobiographical"
in the sense that he wrote it.

Carlo let loose on the Harlemites;
he flicks the switch of the publishers,
eats cognac, eats champagne,
his Iowan teeth like headlights
from Jay Gatsby's coupé.

Reading for the cigarmakers
is not laughter, and not to be laughed at;
good cigars are a novelty
to tourists, but for quality,
white and black, the best
leaf for the book,
smelt of print,
and away from the print,
stylized segregation.

Housing patterns are to be cashed in on;
Strivers Row are bungalows
compared to plantations;
for immigrants,
just off Ellis Island,
they are goldmines
and golden business.

From the Atlanta Archives
four coattailed *sports*
are about to go out on the road.

Hair parted, not a smoker
in the bunch, Weldon tunes up
his infield for the orchestra:

This is GA; it is a town
Du Bois walks in; commercial peachtree
is not the apple of his eye;
he remembers the Seminoles
above all Indians; railroads
are a checkered experience,
chaingangs, turpentine wards,
bring him the blues. He begins to read in Georgia.

The Caribbean calls to understand
revolution; Garvey gets to town
just in time; in Niagara, over the falls,
the braintrust works out strategy.
In eighty years we'll be ready to tackle
Latin America; *Plessy* v. *Ferguson*
is barely cold. The marshals of progress
turn their phases on stock prices;
the stock is paper or it's meat.

Archives

Cooperstown, N.Y.

Photos and clippings fade;
no one can find a real signature
of Rube Foster, who put together
the Negro Leagues; efforts
at why Josh Gibson died at thirty-
five are even vaguer,
his sleek strong body in the waves
of San Juan the vintage year:
1934. Later, 72 home runs,
the only ball over the third tier
at Yankee Stadium
for the games on off-days.

No flicks of Gibson as a Globe-
trotter, his golden gloves
astride the mound captured,
for real, with Curt Flood,
eating steaks on a grill,
in a parking lot in spring
training. Reggie is a mask,
astride a roadster, a paltry
lid on a rainday with Vida Blue.

Frank Robinson's loaded automatic
put him under arrest; the flick
of his headrag, a white mop,
only shown in Cincinnati,
eating Satchel's 45-lb. catfish,
chasing "Willmont" Liquors, Inc.
as endorsements in Brooklyn.

The clippings of the rest
of Negro America are full of glee;
no ounce of bitterness,
except for Jackie, who hit
better than they thought,
and was fast, stealing home
in public, voting Republican,
the whole Civil War
on his back and pigeon-toes.

On PBS the documentaries,
one trailer sideshow,
a whole hall of oral history
in transcriptions
of black and white.

Trujillo, who paid the best,
threatened execution if you lost;
the black World Series in Comiskey
full of chicken, zoot suits,
trainfare from everywhere
but endorsements, turnstyles.

"Let's play two."

Jest: A Collection of Records

Adrift on the porch, chain-smoking,
you'd never believe the seven hours
in the garden, and last night a frost
in June; we could sit down and comfort
you, hear tales of drink,
how you gave up alcohol, the trombone
festering in your hands in Akron, New York.

When you started collecting, the seat
of the house went wet with humidity,
for the basement is jacked up with posts,
and the walls are fortified with books.
We go through your sections
as a symphonist, blind in one eye,
the whole back of the head the trumpet
section. On "Potato Head Blues"
you put away the handkerchief,
tell the black kids on campus
the soul is in technique, to sound
the instrument with the tongue
and let the ear walk about in the garden.

So many blossoms to comfort you in the short
summer; two freezers full of plants
that almost stop your emphysema,
Lucia about to go mad with your schematic
of songs, 45,000 records
holding the house up right next to a greenhouse
where you curry the young tomatoes
before the foot in the ground.

I heard your voice coming from Syracuse
on the first night in town, late January,

the place adrift in snow, the lake effect
nesting the town in sheets of frost
for the way to the farmhouse.

"What Did I Do to Be So Black and Blue"
was the song on the college FM,
your history lesson of how rhythm
was carried by drums, progressing to bass
fiddle, while the repertoire of the saints
disappeared. When I drank from a mug
full of beer with "Slave" and two bare
feet on either side of the grass,
I knew you were an Americana, your shapeless
rolled-up flag on the corner, right next
to the poetry collection, first editions
you read for the soreness in your back
before you went out to plant and harvest.

You end up, once more, on the porch,
a welcome table comes into view,
your stylus and crewcut reminding me
of uncut novels in the irises
going slowly to sleep in rows you sifted
like tobacco, a painted landscape
with a golf course on the borders
of your backyard.

        You would never get
in the cart they sent for you,
dressed up in a tie in midsummer
so you could play in the tight sections
of a tight stairway
        where Bert Williams
danced up a flight of stairs
catching the mouse that left the house
of "The Empty Bed Blues."

—*For Bob Blackmore*

Josh Gibson's Bat

Doubleday Field,
Cooperstown, N.Y.

Empty at the corners,
the crowd bunched up
behind the backstop,
the screen, not high enough
for pop flies,
is crawling with kids,
not a ginger-colored coach
or resident,
on either foul line.

My kid, the first baseman,
with a pro mitt
and a hand-carved bat
made of ash
without his initials,
measures for the fences—
He's got his 34s
and is mad,
half the day spent
in front of coffin's corner,
replicas of the Negro Leagues,
and two hours in archives
looking at photos,
the thickest of Mays
and Jackie,
and they have his bat.

He remembers being called "Sambo,"
as his grandfather was
near Hamilton,
on the IBM Field in Oneonta;
he goes three for three
from the southpaw figures of speech
on the black-and-white scoreboard.

Like his ancestors
he's got a great sense of humor
but not the body of Mays,
too many tapes of Stevie Wonder,
the broad grin of Durocher
protecting him from the girls
who hide in the bleachers.

He figures to tool his bat
with the birthdates of these girls;
he says he cares about color,
the race music of his talk
in the tape-measured records
of the Group Areas Act
unwritten in tar and feathers,
a stand of buttermilk
and a fly stirring the batter
for pancakes in the wrong country.

Hinton's Silkscreens

"On defense he was a hurricane out of bounds."

He goes after paint with soft palms,
the pigment of the iris, heart of gold;

on state buildings he leaves an imprint,
on the gridiron the broken bones of pennants.

Columbus, Georgia, in this trek, is the mill
where the sacks for grain are sewn;

after the bus incident, his people squeezed
into the bump seat in weary rigor mortis,

his father sells the weekend Model A—
even without gas, or good tires, the price

of the ticket is a Tank Factory—
he, a boy of two, is left with his grandmother.

The rivets of his teachers he places in the palms;
he mends in the off-season—at movies comes alive

in frames of motion, stills in black and white,
and in the neighborhoods, where his parents move,

he learns the skills of anger in the soft-spoken
gerunds of the upper registers, lands in Iowa.

Welfare, when one is eligible, is a sack of sugar,
a sack of flour; living underground he props

water leaks, walks the art bridge. In Canada
his sports column is like the brick wall

he once leaped on the stadium runway. In Canada,
you could cup the flesh of the provinces

and not sell your soul every day, though the circuit
of teams had its quota, and its tolls.

Did you ever see the two pickaninnies on the front
porch of Mrs. Stowe's memorial house while you went to school?

Hillcrest Cemetery held its arms wide open
for the black faces from the cramped bus

you escaped from, the parts line of the conveyor
built in the fever of perpetual war.

On a spare holiday, in Mexican waters, the reef
produced more than children, though you made them

tow the line of the horizon, in race relations,
and in black and white, unmentionables on canvas.

Your soft hands calm animals, medicine for sleepy eyes,
which droop and glisten in the panic of winds, and daylight.

Conversations with Roy DeCarava

You have to pay him for a rerun
of the videotape, $5 for a single feature:
"All the things you are"
you are:
        what is the function of light?
and how to see?

For a boy on the street in 1920
you don't need art supplies,
some colored chalk for hopscotch,
the pigeon-toed balls of the feet.

On a Guggenheim you don't figure
a white dress on a black woman's wedding
day is really subject matter
for the *Family of Man,*
but she enters the shadow anyway.

Was the coffee-can lens
you made into an enlarger
Maxwell House?

At Cooper Union no names were called,
nothing called back as you went uptown,
in the shadows
the high hat of the drumset
too out of balance to adjust,
too sweet for the accents of color.

Full Tones: a fool for expression,
the hues of the neighborhood,
a social self steeped in the luck
of life force, the vital music.

To see some fingers on a man
like Coltrane or Bags;
the long exquisite glassmakers
of exorcism,
the black hole of Kamoinge.

At the Studio Museum you're alive
at tuxedo junction, Sherry your corsage;
in the shadow is the bicycle,
files of negatives in the basement,
and in the open spaces of the Savoy,
dancers where "Lester Leaps In."

The Beauty Shell

—*In memoriam:*
   Bernice Lewis Clark, 1914–90

—*For Bernard Bruce, Sr.*

In the rinse
the straightening
or letting go wild

there is the undulating
hat, parapet for fresh flowers,
where all beauty sits

on the head,
but one must watch feet
and hands in all weather.

My son, Bernard,
has just called the shop;
he is late for dinner

which he will prepare
after long jumps,
the furlongs he savors

at the BU stadium,
a long procession
down Mass. Ave.

right in front of the shop
if he should jump out of the pit
(and with his luck

into the fire or a frying pan)—
a good boy though
and a good man

with streamlined
temper, weakness
for the ladies

not all of them
in the shop
by any means.

He has fought
university poverty

and easy solutions
for the victims

with equal weight
and diligence;

has fought the impulse
not to lie

to superiors
and friends alike,

has talked his way
in and out of contracts

with the devil
who often parades

in a cap & gown
at convocation

and commencement:
has tried to raise

his children as himself
perennials for cultivation.

He is his own hairstyle,
happy and almost bald
with finely shaped tome
of his father,
who never turned out "all here";

it is not his fault, the boy,
who liked to fish
and garden
with few tools
and could mend or build

anything he had to live in.
Once he had to return
two suits and a topcoat
with the wrong labels
at Filene's—

that boy could shop
with the best of them—
    loved gold and jewelry
for his oblong hands
he would not wear

in gloves or sleeves.
He made good babies
in the best habit,
raising them
as embroidery

to crescent and crochet,
for I have taught them all
to knit.
Next life I will turn
every wall into a milliner's

display case,
wear each chapeau
to church, a dance,
or a wedding,
and every hat from my own hand.

Fixit

—In memory of Lester Young, master innovator, tinkerer,
magician of profane conceits: Pres!

So tired of trains and buses
we went back to planes,
Pres walks up to "Lady Flip"
with a bent rod;
the sex of the episode
is already in ballads,
little room for interpretation
except when you're rested.

Flip puts Pres out
of the back room,
begins straightening his rod,
just one bad one,
the wire on the plane
condensed to nothing,
a low B-flat
now tangible on Pres's
tongue and jowls.

He ain't no cat you've ever
tempted with fish for dinner;
he's somebody with range,
and now able to read
charts and scores
with utter abandon.

Doors open with that B-flat;
you can hear the hush of breezes
with flickering light
on Flip's tools:

"My people won't play
without you."

Changes on Coleman "Bean" Hawkins's Birthday

—For Robert Burns Stepto,
   and in memory of his parents

Piano at four, cello at seven,
then the saxophone.

I saw a picture of that homestead
in St. Joe; angles in all directions.

Up the road, where the state college in Maryville
stands, they lynched a man for rape.

The poet wonders what effect this had
on Coleman's family, Bean born in '04, lynching bee in '31:

he was probably in Europe; wonder why?
When he returns in '39

the gangplank is full of musicians
waiting for European news.

"Hawk" is grinning, and without asking
figures he'll be in a monstrous duet

uptown, with his nemesis,
Herschel Evans.

                    He doesn't bother to think
about "Blue & Sentimental"

with Pres on alto, playing Goodman's clarinet
which the King had given him

after Lester cut him dead in downtown Chicago.
But it was Herschel that had that broad

solo on "B&S"—solo broad as the ocean,
and rough, its edges, even in calm seas,

feasting of competition. For about a day
nobody tells Bean Herschel is gone.

Then the famous recording of "Body & Soul,"
all for Herschel; Pres walked away

poet of his generation, "capping" on his pardners
who abandoned melody, forgot the copious lyrics.

The poet remembers this is Voltaire's
300th anniversary.

He proceeds to think, deeply, about *Candide.*
Such is the birthday of a traveler in Paris

where Hawk has been to, treated *royally.*

Napoleon said "the fifth element was mud."

Dexter Leaps In

"There's not enough kindness in the world."
—from *'Round Midnight*

—*In memory of Dexter Gordon*

An ash, a maple
flowering near Moody's
"last train to Overbrook"
on the plantations
of the vertical: harmonic
modulations of tone,
hairpiece and scapula
of church choirs,
resonant, off-beat blues.

You were sweet-humored,
could kick in any register,
but the horizontal measures,
the melody,
your tufted face
as speech in Ella's favorite song,
those were encumbrances
if clutching was Jug
and Bean in collusion;
as for Trane, an ancestor
in transition
from the immaculate melody
to vertical exposures.
Bud was there because he wanted to be
("Glass Enclosures")—Pres wanted to talk
about Herschel Evans

but this was the Renaissance Club on Sunset Boulevard,
a tandem of wife and kids,
we were happy in the postcoital
post office scheme
of big band admirers, just off "graveyard,"
without a moment's notice to the police,
who were prancing in the alley
making our connections, the moneybags,
the jungle of chaos which was smack,
wilderness of trees
in the woodshed of prison:
sonics, for keeps, on *'Round Midnight.*

Happiness was not the booking agents;
the Watts local was gone, ogres
of the freeway are our battle stations,
so Wardell Gray was there to meet you,
and Stitt, conquering Bird's tunes
in duplication—you went far ahead
on the IUD of the cabaret card:

to live and die on your instrument,
that was exploration
in the hemispheres, the hero's melodies,
the saga, acres of kindness in belief.

You could lose your voice, all things
shut down except the vectors:
"Straight, No Chaser,"
"Well, You Needn't"
planets in the yesterdays
of exile, penitentiary pleasure:
"All the Things You Are."

Fanny's Kitchen

"Every appearance in nature corresponds to some state of mind. . . ."
—Ralph Waldo Emerson

Even you couldn't find space
for the elevator in Burma;
we are all in camps
in this war;
your letter to Langston
is no Iowa winter—
breath of fresh air
in the manner of Weldon Johnson,
who stood before Jubilee Hall
hearing all the family names
in panatellas of disremembrance.

Some chose the blues in big bands,
offshoots of cadenzas and chili;
Grace Nail gave my grandmother
a rocking chair to rock her baby boy;
Langston's poems hung in the vestibule
in Brooklyn, with the Dodgers
knocking heads in Ebbets Field.

They wouldn't let you play the lead,
drove the author of *Glass Menagerie*
into the Iowa River, which ran between huts
on either side of the barracks;
the sun in Rome made you freckle
in cracked Italian
like a vase with sunflowers gleaming
on the smell of hocks.

In Perugia a girl from Norway
beat an errant solicitor
to his knees with her briefcase,
on her way to classes, at 8 A.M.

The eyelids of binoculars catch
jackleg basketball, wrens and terns
going upriver to the bridge:
you could hang a necklace of awards
on Vermont license plates,
where your ship came in;
already, without an apron or a pantry,
you're stroking out to meet it.

"Dixie Peach"

"He was a paperboy; he delivered——."

"Andy" is what the curator
at the local Lawrence Museum
called you, a work of art
in miniature without a photo;
she was too occupied
to be wary of her impudence,
and how could she know
we had just left the blockprint
memento of a pogrom, American
fashion, to Quantrill's raiders,
who had a list of 12
citizens of Kansas,
and could find only bystanders,
a squad of black recruits
who could not hide near the river-
grass, and so were butchered.

Langston didn't look like that;
"Amos 'n' Andy" were props for Simple
at the barstool, and Grandma,
the Reids, St. Luke's AME,
the crafted homestead mortared
in this segregated town,
and you a screen apart
in kindergarten.
                Letters to Mrs. Ames,
mistress at Yaddo, apologize
for the inconvenience of HUAC,
which made its inquiries

at Hadie's kitchenette,
and you sought shelter
at the racetrack,
by watching grooms cool down
Citation, and morning walks
the prettiest in Saratoga,
because those black girls
earned their money riding bareback.

The pomade which glossed your raven
luxurious mop in early grades
was shampooed in race rituals
of the stage, and in your memoirs:
what you hid from us was promise,
rivers on the Solomon,
settlements like Nicodemus,

Kansas, with water of its own.

Saint Sassy Divine

So many facelifts in the middle
registers, sweet contralto serenade;
you came to attention when you read
the riot squad with Brownie,
swift, accident-prone, Clifford Brown.
He could match your timbre,
learning to drive and follow
the curves and banks of turnpike.
You could pigeon-toe the keys
of the choir in Newark.

Nobody spoke when you appeared at the Apollo:
"God had to have his lead singer,"
was all Eckstine said at the end.

The end. Movie, or brief hit
on the charts of television;
early, when you had your doubts
about contests, you broke your face
with lifts, as though the height
and weight of middleweight champion
of this world and the next
was never enough.

Then there was "Lush Life";
vibrato to break your heart
from sonar to scrotum.

You bore children on the stage
as you sweat bullets in klieg lights
of affection, our immaculate bop diction,
your choice of words in silhouette.

"The friends I have had sad and sullen
gray faces, with distant gay traces;
if you could be there you could see
where they'd been washed away by too
many through the day: 12 o'clocktails";
that was after-hours; you were all-musician
in the practice sessions; nobody
could figure out your favorite flower,
it was not gardenias, or the circus rose,
but sable was your color, and mink,
the combat of the dross, the viaduct,
the bridge, content in quiet costume.

Then there was Los Angeles; up La Brea
in the fog to lady marijuana
didn't have the least effect on your lungs.
You could sing for starters,
a bumblebee with effortless plummage
inoculating our village gardens,
and our latrines.

How you felt about the South, grand
tours that turn archives
into the chicken shacks on Route 66,
are still in your love of clothes:
the animals of the world,
cheetah, gazelle, armadillo,
covered your back and thighs
like lacquer, like Wild Turkey.

You were boss in the kitchen
when you cooked for piano players:
Cole was best in the alcove,
one could never get away from Tatum,
Hampton Hawes was scared of you
when you opened your mouth.

Strings were effervescent;
when we christened you as champagne
lady of the decade, every decade,

we spoke of verbal plumage,
silks etched and rolled by the gods.

And God did speak at reception
when the healing song began:

alone and aware
at my picnic table

in the St. Francis Hotel
in San Francisco
I could not afford,
you sang to us
in our tense fragility
of sorrows as we grew.

Autographs won't do;
wages misspent in recordings;
on FM you have stopped traffic
with "Tenderly"
in the redlight district.

Inside your bosom,
in the light of the elevator
was the cervix/larynx
and meter for the biggest bands;
the caustic trio
incomplete without your nails,
the ball mike collapsed,
brittle, salient octaves,
the gamefish in ethereal
waters for the firehorse
of surrender, of sainthood,
if the saint was congress,
a wakeful gorgeous child.

The child walks on water
in the sign of Pisces,
uncontested *God's Trombone.*

FOUR

~

Laureate Notes

Teaching Institutes

We have this on video
so performance is tendentious
as teachers are
in the wee hours of their torment
for to be clear and impassioned
is not a daily event,
and preparation, the wise reading
and talk with the ancestors,
is never-ending,
divine conversations
on the rims of the pit.

You don't need another talk
on plurality; the feminists
among you can count amendments,
know the patrons of the canon,
can deed the script;
the American tongue is ongoing,
its Spanish equivalents
in the turkey camps
across diminishing farmlands,
as though you yourself
can afford not to eat
having raised food
against famine all your lives.

Famine is what we talk about,
for the camera of the feast
is posturing, an eloquent
gravitation away from the vote,
away from administration.

What we do administer:
our hopes, of course,
a better life, a job with promise
at the end of the road;
all beginnings are possible:
race and gender and age
talking and gender and age
talking to each other on camera.

But alone there is winter;
you must cover your tracks
to the igloo, the cabin
in the middle of the city.

You are homeless here;
you will pay with the life of the book.

Laureate Notes

—*To the* Providence Journal

Four papers a day, *Globe, Times,*
Monitor are not enough,
this is a personal editorial,
this is demise. Update your photo
gallery; all the black people do not
appear in the negative, and in broad
daylight, let's say, on Broad Street,
a rainbow, a cliché, but a full range
of coloration.
          Which is your slant
on dry and wet news, please, give
us the facts; save the attitudes
for the collection plate,
which in the old days,
was a hammer, a trestle,
and a boy in the dark
unable to make change
because he was folding the news,
in the hot, in the cold.

Your police news lacks how you treat
the rich, how you make fun of
immigrants, who count out their
change in the women's room,
which is often out of paper:
this is the paper of the numbers,
this is the paper of the rich.

I will not comment on the police:
they are brown, sometimes on horses,
and often patrol: my boy watched you chase
a 15-year-old up Chestnut Street
in a heisted car, and, when he lost
control, watched him beaten into
submission, and because he was upstairs,
and not at ground level,
with a perfect view for justice,
and my answers, which came quickly,
because he stutters, looks Cape Verdean,
has been hassled by men in brown
for their amusement.

I realize these men have their own children;
I realize they are not in love with mine;
when it comes to protection, editors,
one must get one's blows in early,
if you want to make sense
to a kid about justice,
about the law.

This is one or two incidents,
it must stand for the whole;
it is all he knows about order,
it is all he speaks of the law.

Tomorrow: car theft; tomorrow: trash
collection; tomorrow: judges and juries;
tomorrow: the IRS, BVA, MLA, PAL, CVS, NBC, BRU
tomorrow: happened today.

Mule

"The black woman is the mule of the world."
—Zora Neale Hurston

*Mulatto: "the offspring of a mule donkey and a mare
used esp. as a beast of burden because of its patience,
sure footedness, and hardiness; colloq.: a stupid or
stubborn person; a machine which spins cotton into
yarn and winds onto spindles; a kind of slipper
which leaves the heel exposed."*

Whereas the donkey neighs its ardor,
imitating the mule and the horse,
this donkey calls up Cape Verde,
connections betrothed to South
African Airlines, hop-on-point
to the New World,
and the old country.

Tutu snoozes in the semigloss
of her eyedrops; when she wakes
to her children's commotion
your father, Tony, is still alive,
and in his habit of work
and play, an image of safety:
(he is the found safety net)

You will be that man!
Aloof, even on Benefit Street,
feinting your limbs for hook
and palette, carrying your own
tempo as toolshed of glorious
composition, your pastels
are precious tintypes, for miracles

abound in the poverty of Fox Point,
such poverty over fish & bakery,
such poverty in the eyes of Tutu.

Your good manner, easy mirth,
composure, grace, these qualities
of heartbreak, pivot in the mind:

the nude with light all around
her ventricles as candles of sacrifice,
is splendid, the child, easy
and alive in the glow,
that is striven for, Michael,
the dream of *being* oxygen again:

to make is to start over
on the carpet of the sacred,
in the stomach of a grown man.

The steel of its purpose,
alloy to carry everything within us
on paper, wood, granite, puddin' rock,
to make it sing
in the cavity of the heart:
the mule levitates in service.

And we have burdened it,
our temperament, at its best,
compliant, easeful, ready to perform;
like the pig to be eaten
on the slab, in the pit,
where we are now, Tutu,
shifting our load, salving our bedsores,
still afraid, in tenacity, for prayer.

—*For Alberto Torres Pereira*

Manong: Angola

"This is not the way I was supposed to live."

Oil and diamonds
afloat in black markets,
Unita, the government,
in the heart of madness,
Luanda Central Hospital,
"Domingo," I whisper.
Who has eaten dogs,
cats, rats,
grasshoppers,
is blind from hunger,
and as he rocks
in the darkness
he swats flies.

All are conscripting
fifteen-year-olds,
and one without anesthetic,
screams in groin shrapnel,
screams in black market places,

which is South Africa,
which is the patois
of money, for power,
our poetry of exchange
in life and death.

All is paid in dollars.

—*For Anani Dzidzienyo*

Rhode Island (SSBNT740): A Toast

—For the Christening of the USS Rhode Island

Majestic, sullied, sultry
in invention, we should never forget
it has teeth, its new log and sleeve
like all its sisters, Katy
bars the door, or opens it,
and we are in a new age at sea,
and by the shore in august bird
of egress in its pioneer charts,
for we must wait for noise
and benediction,
honors given and taken
at departure in the minutiae
of bells.
In daylight,
evaporating in sonar, lozenges
of the inner ear of the crew
are bonded by provision,
by protocol, and an invisible
flag, which cannot come to quantum
attitude until force
is out of the cave
whose weaponry is its religion.

At the helm, the quiet rigor,
tested samplings of logistics,
determined wind eating the air
where no eagle will ever land,
we are at command to strategic
flagrant good, and we will play

percentages on the return,
and on the watch.
At night,
the seascape above us,
we shall repeat the code,
and the message of the state:
prepare to be merciful
in cunning power;
this is the zone of freedom.

The Sanctity of the Unwritten

Taught to be glib
on time
patient
all things unnatural,
you traverse papers
morning news
background music
to the fact
wrecking crew
as deadly
as carcinoma.

With a change of clothes
in the office closet
and facemasks
of words in books
you glide
in the space
inertia calls
without a song.

Suddenly
as the tree
inside you
without water,
the roots
only as deep
as your groin

you have nothing to say.

As in framed tales from the ancients
you begin saying it
in your head

best place for it

nothing for the mandible
of the page.

Mr. Knowlton Predicts

I line up all the books he has treated
in goatskin, and with his nimble elan,
how he solves the framing of that I love:
words arranged in blossoms
forever at ease in their flowering,
and words of remorse, of patience,
of the coming flood.
                          We stagger,
on this day, among his tools,
all the implements of family,
and how he came to fly
over the capital city
with Lindbergh,
and came back undiminished
by height, weight,
and his mastoid condition,
which made him the captain
of the book, and the box
that contains the book.

He built himself his own silo
with bricks, adrift in the sun,
and in the rain a garden,
for even a small farm
in the backyard
on the homestead
in Bristol
is an oasis
when it comes to Nina.

And when it comes to the book
he teaches in the dark,
easy as his laughter,
which is spontaneous,
and not without pain.

Go through the pain
he says with his techniques
of the bound word,
Italian, Egyptian, Narragansett,
Kru: we are alive again
in all that made us,
remodeling the bindings,
thread, pristine paper,
in the root cellar of his art.

Madam Tutu

"—And Maria's name was called out by the M.C.—
'Maria Da Luz Pereira Ramos.' She rises and walks
across the dance floor to receive her prize. She walks in
splendid solitude across the floor; her walk is a dance, a
morna. She is 500 years old and older. Silver bracelets
jangle on her wrists; a necklace glitters at her throat; her
ancestors sleep under her skin. She carries Cape Verde
in her left arm; she carries Africa in her right arm. Per-
fect grace, beauty, pride strength. Maria glides. 'But see
that woman of Cape Verde; old, beautiful. Yes!'"

> —From *Songs in a Secret Language,*
> by Alberto Torres Pereira

"Her mouth was . . . open, but her breathing took up so
much of her strength that she could not talk. But she
looked at me, or so I felt, to speak for her. . . ."

> —From Zora Neale Hurston's account of her last
> encounter with her dying mother, found in a
> chapter entitled "Wandering" in her autobiography,
> Dust Tracks on a Road (1942)

—For Alberto Torres Pereira and Family

Maria Ramos—"Tutu"; *anya tutu:*
"do you remember Antonio, Tony Pereira"—
he studies the bed, chair,
"do you know me, Tutu?"
She crochets her hem,
her down eyelids closed,
her glasses, impervious
to the light of her reflection,
about to fall in her lap—
"sit with me awhile."

Do you remember where we lived? Do you know
Virginia? Dingley Court;
do you remember your sons, daughter,
what are their names?
what is my name? Dingley Court,
where my father died?

Tilts, in fine measure of remembrance,
the well-kept profile and chin,
eyes closed, her glasses,
now on the shelf,
this shelf too intricate for seeing.

"You left too early, Alberto"—She knits,
answers to "How's Mary?" as an aide,
the delicate one with power to spare
for any movement, abating body sores,
muscle spasms, wheelchair light.

Albert feels the wall; sometimes it is a glass
wall, brilliant in overtures of creosote,
nitrate, amber-blue, sometimes translucent,
as a good shade, handmade, from home.

"It is after 7 P.M.; she is in her own
place, tired; come earlier, Alberto,
come tomorrow:
Tutu will know you tomorrow."

What of her place where nothing reaches her
but surrender: that is where
two Marys converse—
The blessed one, the profane keeper,
who bathes our master
without diaphanous muslin.
That, Alberto,
is the wall of transcendence:
that is Tutu's sacred place.

The Ghost of Soul-making

*"On that day it was decreed who shall live and
who shall die."*
　　—Yom Kippur prayer

"Art in its ultimate always celebrates the victory."

The ghost appears in the dark of winter,
sometimes in the light of summer, in the light
of spring, confronts you behind the half-door
in the first shock of morning,
often after-hours, with bad memories to stunt
your day, whines in twilight, whines in the umbrella of trees.

He stands outside the locked doors, rain or shine;
he constructs the stuntwork of allegiances
in the form of students, in the form of the half-measure
of blankets—he comes to parade rest in the itch of frost
on the maple, on the cherry caught in the open field
of artillery; he remembers the battlefields of the democratic
order; he marks each accent through the gates of the orchard
singing in the cadences of books—
you remember books burned, a shattering of crystals,
prayers for now, and in the afterlife, Germany of the northern
lights of Kristallnacht, the ashes of synagogues.

The ghost turns to your mother as if he believed
in penance, in wages earned, in truth places these flowers
you have brought with your own hands,
irises certainly, and the dalmation rose,
whose fragrance calms every hunger in religious feast or fast.
Into her hands, these blossoms, her fragrant palms.

There is no wedding ring in the life of ghosts,
no sacred asp on the wrist in imperial cool,
but there is a bowl on the reception table,
offerings of Swiss black licorice.
On good days the bowl would entice the dream
of husband, children, and grandchildren;
on good days one could build a synagogue in one's own city,
call it *city of testimony, conscious city of words.*
In this precinct male and female, the ghost commences, the ghost
    disappears.

What of the lady in the half-door of the enlightenment:
tact, and a few scarves, a small indulgence for a frugal
woman; loyalty learned in the lost records of intricate relations:
how to remember, how to forget the priceless injuries
on a steno tablet, in the tenured cabinets of the files.
At birth, and before, the ghost taught understanding:
that no history is fully a record, for the food we will eat
is never sour on the tongue, lethal, or not, as a defenseless
scapegoat, the tongue turned over, as compost is turned over,
to sainthood which makes the palate sing. These are jewels
in the service of others; this is her song. She reaps
the great reward of praise, where answers do not answer,
when the self, unleashed from the delicate bottle,
wafts over the trees at sunrise and forgives the dusk.

—*For Ruth Oppenheim*

E.J.M. at 75

"It is late at night and still I am losing."
—Robert Frost

The senator remembers
Waterloo, Iowa,
where his black friend
was ridden
out of town from St. Paul.

He could stand on a fence
if he wanted to,
for religion is a rail-
splitting industry
in Minnesota.

In Watkins,
baseball, terrible
odors from the sky,
and up north,
great fishing
on ancestral boundary homelands.

He has learned this
over beef
in Chicago,
and stood up against
HUAC's arsenal
when he didn't have tenure.

Tenurable offenses
are closest to memory:
Lincoln's best idea
was colonization,

if expediency
ruled today's obstinacy,
even the best minds

withdrawing from the flesh;

and embracing it.

He takes hold in his daughter's
perch in the nearby graveyard,
ministered by celestial starlings.

He pays with his wit,
he pays with his antlers
which are unruly,
subject to hidden laws
of the poet,
or the tambourine man.

Songs of equity
won't leave him to go
through this wilderness
or that plowed field.

He thinks of the Irish
patrician poet
without indulgences;
he thinks in solitaire
as he reads the sacred
documents,
not as lawyer
or Indian chief (Cherokee),
but as a man with letters,
reading from left to right,
right to left.

Across the campuses
the 60's are topical seminar
in idle commission:
it is a young country,
forgetful in its
terrible flight.

We are quick to kill
the messenger,
quaintly crossing the colorline,
in sanctuaries and graveyards,
where the best trees,
maples, with deciduous fruit,
topple and glow.

—*For Eugene J. McCarthy, on his birthday,*
  29 March 1991

FIVE

~

Honorable Amendments

Advice to Clinton

"The prayers of both could not be answered—that of neither has been answered fully."
    —Abraham Lincoln, from his second inaugural address

Reread A. Lincoln's 2nd Inaugural:
ethical schizophrenia stifles us;
educate; under disguise sit in on
immigration parade—keep handy
your enrichment—define "Arkansas
Traveler" as clinical care,
"the old" substance masquerading anew.

Pardons (from A. Lincoln)

The Christmas tribe, in the big city,
is forgiven; what they did, what people
actually committed the crime, who is guilty,
that is contained in the pardon,
written in long-hand, before the Emancipation
Proclamation, and the Sioux
are unreconciled to events.
They stand, each in his own deathsong,
on the group platform for justice,
every one guilty of being a Dakota,
the sundance of retribution in the pen.

"Due Process" is for 38 braves
who are wasted on the knees and backbones
of the citizens of New Elm;
in the bakery in Mankato
there is a powwow of forgiveness
in the leavened bread,
but no one remembers the 38
who were not guilty
and Dakota still avoid Mankato in all seasons.

It is said that the 38 eagles
circling above the powwow
were the grandfathers of the eagles—
"Now there are eagles on the ground."

In "Land of Memories" Park
the pipe ceremony honors the ancestors;
the victors write their history
on National Public Radio, though rites
of legal protection are suspended,

as the knots on the guillotine-platform
one hundred twenty-five years ago in New Elm.

There was "no time for a defense";
symbolic pardons are unofficial.
At Hardee's the machine fast food
are the new gallows of "Sleepy Eye"
and "Little Crow," nesting places
for eagles that flew over the regional
library when research was done.
The sculptor made a limestone report
for the village elders; they sing
into existence the world where song belongs,
songlines, aboriginal songs,
a roadway of connections
with the world of existence.

No gallows can speak for eagles
of the president's quill pen.

Godfather

Born off an alley
in the Shaw district—
certainly not Colonel Shaw
of "Glory";

died in his pajamas
on the can—
no music
when they found him;

"Sunday Morning"—
his face
on the bathtub,
a left temple bruise.

A dude, even
in the old days,
at Dunbar,
Howard;

docent in his twilight:
theatrical: loved live
performance.

In love with my mother,
my uncle's friend,
and so, with his manners,
never got over that love,
didn't speak of it,
though I wear his cufflinks
and pins
from his tuxedo.

We were in the Sheraton,
he'd forgot his medication,
held all he knew at the time
in the fine knuckles of one hand;
this was right after Christmas,
colder in the nation's
capital than any museum.

Docents, when young,
recite the facts;
as they grow older,
improvise.

Those knuckles, select jewelry
from every tradition,
style at the wave of a hand,
buried, not far from here:
"one more colored regiment
in the soul of a man."

—*For Charles Miles, 1908–90*

Studs

Off-color eyes that shine through lobes,
the flesh still uneaten by stickpin,
he was stuck to her; this attachment,
like string from the loops of IUD
caught him unawares, in planes
above the Earth, on plains
near the homestead, on water
which he has touched with his belt
and bow, as a lifeguard,
before he met her.
                        Yes, she could brown
in that sun, the broad shoulders
concealed in flesh for his children,
who grew beyond her; he built a shed
for her tools, the garden, the chain saw—
windows faced toward the southern estuary
where turtles called, for the pond
swelled in the porous ground,
from springs, and she was a spring.

All day he has thought of Seminoles;
all day he has dreamed of the Narragansett;
his children could fit in if the drum
were opened to shells he could use
for the dinner table, and shells
from the sea decorate the walls
of the uterus, mystery of caves
he got lost in on special dates,
January 15 for instance,
now a national holiday;
and April 23, her father's birthday,

and Shakespeare's,
where he read in a long line
at the Library of Congress
after visiting the Capitol
where Martin Luther King, Jr.
stood in consummate black stone.

Now he must ask about diamonds;
how refraction turns into bloodlines
he could choose for band music,
the territory bands
of Count Basie, without charts,
in a beat-up van,
passing for Indians,
passing in the slow lane
through the culture.

He would place her flesh there;
he would ask her to wear these,
diamond studs, in each ear,
to hear his song: to hear his name
come alive in her ears.

My Father at 75

He makes his own soup from scratch;
by the watch he does crossword, cleanup
and the stationary bicycle;
if allowed to he lives in the past
but the phone, news, and memoirs
tabulate and afflict him.

He was born in a small town
and still is uncomfortable
with his people;
discomforture hones standards.
He refuses to budge.

I like his attire when he flies,
pressed jacket and slacks,
a few papers, his walking shoes;
I have seen the women of the world
make passes at him directly to his face;
my mother would laugh at this:

get yourself a young Mexican,
make fire steam from my daughter's nose.

I don't ask about the neighborhood
or prospects south of the border,
but when he walks his innings at dawn
I walk with him.

    La Brea is not the tarpits
but the bottom of a hill where my brother
did a blind cutaway, with his helmet on,
on the right lane pavement,
blindsided by a woman in a Continental.

After two weeks it was him that gave the word
to unplug him. On the next street
lived a childhood friend who's disappeared;
he has the face of many abused children
anxious to please, on crack or benzedrine,
for his face is cracked by the fruit
of camouflage, and betrayal:
he did not bury his parents
or let them rest in an urn.

This is the street of weights; it is a system
of barbells and pulleys in anxious backyards;
it is the nectar of barking dogs on chains;
there are parked cars everywhere and license
plates from the Caribbean, from Quantico Bay.

We will not go on from here; we will return
to the ivy, and the digging, and when the rains
come, to watering in the early hours.
He will feed the dogs at dusk. And let them go.
Portraits of the world, which was my mother, and her children,
caress and afflict him. He has the neat
penchant of a man who contends to stay home.

Protégé: 1962

—In memory of Dorothy Parker

In the front row
and big as a house
the kid sits there
waiting for the word;

he gets it from a crow,
a broken-winged woman
who needs a drink,
and he comes to her aid

because she can't talk—
too frightened to speak.
He goes up to put his arm,
the tight shirt of his bicep

like rings of a telephone
booth where he gets her to speak.
She comes alive
in the Algonquin,

which is no place
for any lady
without text in Los Angeles
should she be found out in class.

She takes the waning
light of a sunset
on the wrong side of the field,
an earthquake

on the continent of gone Indians:
"God ain't always there
when you call on him;
but he's always on time."

Next class session
she's dead;
the bulging boy in his team
shirt begins to read

her few books
to herd the braves
who never talked
to any selves but horses.

The Revolutionary Garden

Hieroglyphics of the mace,
the posture of the faculty,
pose of building and trustee,
janitors come and gone:
the service industry of the deep night
now gatekeepers of deep mines,
facile libraries,
a prominent Abraham Lincoln,
apt phrasing, personal losses,
his mad midwifery of the nation's
cylindrical wounds
of the black feminine persona,
a mindset of Sojourner Truth.

She is suspicious of speech on the run,
the pastel banners crisscrossed
in the oleander lights of the public
square, the flexible fire escape.

The human rite in secret blood
and sinew, the science of defensive
starting phrasing, the idol labs,
their great dorsal fins of circuitry
blooming everywhere,
the not so pure products of America

needs a balancing act on the wintry trapeze,
bigger than Chaplin, more special
than wavering tongues and herringbone,
the necklace of divinity:
we sit down on our prayer rugs
and ubiquitous tea,
in the fuse and muster of the constable

for her heart listens all your life:
she does not sleep on the expedient wishes
of the few, remembering
the child alive in the man,
kissing the direct, crucible in the ark;
this revolutionary garden.

My Father's Face

Schomburg Archives

Over his fastidious hands
his voice breaks,
and because he had executed
the bequest
(typing the book lists
sermons in manuscript
& unlisted artifacts)
on his son's birthday
in the Brooklyn brownstone,
this is a double loss,
unbeknownst, even to him,
at this late date
in the March snow,
how much the past costs;
how much the health
of one's nation
as neighborhood,
is stored in the family,
the archives,
the handwriting
of our saints & sinners,
and the forgiveness
of sin's remembering.
(As for the saints)
For now the ancient folders
are enough for the sorrow,
which is grief over my mother's
life, and the grand thematics

of a little girl,
polishing her jacks
on her grandfather's marble
steps, too close, even for him,
to the Germantown governors
who account for the meal
and his till.

We are here on the edge
of another parade,
a huge mural
as a gate,
east and west,
in honor of Nat Cole's walk,
as if his majesty
on the keyboard,
the lilt of his Montgomery
voice,
was a memorial to running water,
to stone, and the masonry
of singing on the stone,
which was his pledge,
which was his right.

This is the penmanship
of song; we are journalists
for the race this Saturday,
in honor of Saturday's child,
a sacred seat with the father.

Lecturing on a Theme of Motherhood

The news is of camps, outpost, little progress;
I expect a bulletin from you on the latest
police foray into the projects, get it,
equal pay before the law, the only amendment
where angels talk to one another
about Friday, no eagles in evidence,
a few terns, almost broken apart in bottlecaps,
but who manage to fly.

Your grandson, Patrice, is playing basketball
in his football jersey; he says he can't cut
T's lawn because the place is ragged with daffodils—
his first recognition that flowers are the plateau
above the grace. He lays down in the gravel
driveway when asked to do chores, too close
to the free throw line to shoot left-handed,
his natural delusion to your changing my grip
on a spoon at the high chair. I don't remember
the candy, told so often you're bound to forget
disappearance, the odor of shad Aunt Ede would make
after her trip to DeKalb Avenue, holding up traffic,
mind you, with a cane, which she wrapped on the head-
lights of the bus, its white aura frolicking
in the police van driven by her students she knuckled
in the South Bronx, just before it burned down.

My Students Who Stand in Snow

—In memory of M.L.K., Jr.,
4 April 1985

Your tall, fresh faces stand up in the snow,
melt some time later in another scene,
modest springs beneath the grass;
they graze, pummel, take off on wheels,
and drink, in cans and chairs all up for sale.

In every clearing a woman in a wagon takes a ride;
the robin (of hockey) is both puck and wing.

Sirens come off on Fridays when the Post is locked;
they go off in jeans, book jackets, clocks.

Once, on *his* day, we held hands before the chapel,
a few spoke, thirty or more in a looseleaf circle,
two urban boys shaking in their boots;
the boots stood up in their stockings of skin,
turned to parchment, made a chime.

From the open windows (on the green) the wings of others
took their places. When the stroke of April
began to sink in snowbank, mud, daffodil,
the black drake came to swim with the white.

Business came to terms; a sound trumpeted—
scenes of this music in clumsy turf, folds, follows.

Testifying

a church
at the first level
is an echo chamber
its own creation
which we make

As in any sanctified church, menagerie
is home: birds, exotic plants, books
perch on the active mind—when she hosted
lunch, always working lunch but not institutional
fare, it was to read, lecture, and teach
for the students needed an example, and spouses,
and a wary kitchen staff at attention,
ready to be quizzed. One does many shuffles
on the doorstep, up or down, into one's
drawing room, an ongoing conversation,
how to fetch, recall, retrieve: everywhere
there is a Minnesota connection.

Dinner begins with Sheridan scotch, which would
be malt in the categories of high and low barley,
mountain pass, glen; one is always on Sheridan Island.

With that peculiar edge of maternity, husbanding
resources, community work, group entertainment,
she is no day at the beach; like her clothes,
expensive, unobtrusive, preeminently in charge,
she has text, has written it, hones context,
laughs into her mustache, holds back, lofts ahead.

One source of great pain are the rituals of race
and agony to me too, but to her "illiterate,"
as in bookshelf, which she goes to in military speed.

First edition of *Invisible Man,* which is scuffed
with markings of rereading, in hard cover, since
publication: what I take this gift to mean:
thematics of citizenship, bird imagery for flight,
many landing spaces in the seams of the text,
which, like water, is rippling, has a flowchart,
glass, and the rivets of a rocky beach; always
with obligations to feed the young, those who
gauge their educations, in the formal sense, as truncated,
"straight, no chaser" hazard pay, changing the gender
in dialogue, suffering fools, for she had enemies:
who were they?

The territory is within us: sustain, maintain, renew,
populate, enhance, expand, as in menu, cookware, cuisine,
tableware, an accumulation, command decisions, abstract
and in praxis, as in efficacies of command.

You could take orders from this woman; you would like it.

—*In memory of Harriet Waltzer Sheridan, 1925–92*

Thimble

—*For Lois*

My mother loved Philadelphia
because her grandfather
preached there;
"come on, Jack,"
he would say to her sister
when he made his rounds,
and not so often,
when he needed an "Amen,"
from that little girl,
bright as a thimble.

Henrietta, dressmaker-queen
of small sizes
must've known the Simon brothers,
the Welsh immigrants,
so she gave the touch
to my mother, who loved
Mexican silver.

In the glass dome,
your sterling notebook,
tells the comprehensive
story as a memoir
of the underground railroad,
if anyone in this world
wanted the full story.

We are reduced to
"called to meals,"
and glad to get them

having graduated
from gruel to capons.

Still we can lay on
the silver, when we have to:

your newsladen epistles,
over fifty years,
make up the patchwork
of a nation's understory,
birds migrating
as friends,
from the other world.

Crypt

—*In memoriam:*
   Ralph Waldo Ellison, 1914–94

Back from the fingers of a twenty-
year-old Barnard Rapunzel,
raised on your embellished kid tales
upcountry, and a garden too high for Plainfield
to beat the frost, early and late;

then the Bennington gang, chaotic
hollers from the academy and still,
such eloquence as "The Lottery,"
a grand, poetic excuse for ritual;

now Connecticut, where the deep patterns
of liquid science and art combine
in sunsets, river wanderings, bluffs;
you are Tuskegee Airman, gingertype:
the annual football season of patterns
in *Invisible Man,* who, defiantly,
is not the author, leaping from rants
to the bowels of Jack the Bear, a writer
musing, in black & blue, over his memoir.

Overcome 'um with grandfather clauses.
The eagle of the Hudson in *Moby Dick,*
soars in zenith of birds, plunges
in shadows of the caverns, regal forever.

At the end, "who knows but that on the lower
frequencies, I speak for you"; but it's not
over, as chaos reigns in the fictional light
of polity, rainbow, without easy coalition.

the artifact completes personality
You are resting in the cylinder
high above the patio, an empty chamber
for the widow, Fanny, whose gaze will join yours
out over the Hudson on Riverside Drive:
as oven-bird she will rescue those finished pages
from the burning house, unfreezing inertia,
releasing the cowering dog, as the cabin burns.

Trinity Chapel is shabby, invited guests,
the secret press, your brother, friends,
students, in tutelage, and the word comes
from the *committal*
                          stopped dead at four score,
seconds only, a lifetime. And here comes chaos:

A man in a green jacket, with paltry tools,
commands three swarthy, unkempt Hispanic
workman in unlaced Nikes, such ceremony
is little comfort for mourners
    (rollaway dollie grunting in hydraulics)
and must be reminded of that democratic
faith your prose lies in. Poet of invisibility,
framed as Tarp limped in Fred Douglass's remains,
for Douglass's house was set afire in Rochester,
his portrait on the walls of the future,
which was your dream. "You rascal, you," you said
to me; "uphill" to your wondrous Fanny.

You read Patrice's birthday postcard from Bard:
the music of his tears are restless compositions
as he remembers lessons from the pit:
"trained incapacity" as shadow:
blessed is the act.

Parenting

—For J.F.K., Jr.,
and in abiding memory for his mother, Jackie O

1

Cutting class to make rehearsals
of *Playboy of the Western World,*
and caught dead on the front page
of the *Providence Journal*
escorting Brooke Shields,
you come to tell me
you need South African lit.
seminar in English
to graduate—two weeks
from commencement:
"You are going to belong to me,"
I say to you on your foreign bicycle,
and you report on Olive Shreiner's
Story of an African Farm,
of Albert Luthuli's Sharpeville
Massacre commentary,
of Lewis Nkosi, Can Themba,
Percy Qoboza, Nadine Gordimer,
Richard Rive, Bessie Head, Athol Fugard
and when you pass, pass/fail,
you send your mother to Hillel
House to hear my song
for the Kapstein Chair,

one I cannot sit in
as Kappy stands on his
last legs to introduce me.

> *Can't you see*
> *what love and heartache's done to me*
> *I'm not the same as I used to be*
> *this is my last affair*

2

She walks up in iris blue
to thank me for all I've done
for you; says "you have such
beautiful children," as she greets
them all, then, asks about your
character, your sense of narrative,
how voice grows in the body
of the republic, for high or low.

Kappy smiles—he was in Vietnam
in '61—met Diem, was a patriot,
lectured on Coleridge, fought
the pallor of reduction to his sacred
texts, a wayward kid
from Fall River
whose first novel filled the campus
with promise. *And he taught.*

He says   "I'd be proud
to have your refrain from 'Last Affair; . . .'
as my epitaph
on my gravestone."

3

In August he was gone.
My son, Patrice, comes up to me;
he's fourteen—"Now I know why I came
to hear you read, Dad, to meet Jackie O."

Outside of Hillel, across the green,
Senator Kennedy speaks to national
service, to sanctions, to his
brothers, Jack & Bobby, decades gone,
to Reverend King,
to his sister-in-law come home.

Her handshake, bright, luminous,
and strong, is heartfelt.

He remembers one evening
in the Churchill House basement,
the only white in an all-black
seminar on the homelands,
disinvesting in South Africa,
fundraising for Mandela.

He remembers her now
at Arlington
under the arc
of the eternal flame:

he notices, on C-Span,
the only couple of color
in this private good-bye,
the son of the maid,
from the Dominican Republic,
and his wife, a poet, from Yale:
contrary to his posturing,
and the errant editorial,
they act like they belong there,
and they act as they should.

He thinks to himself
in the retinue of the mace,
the preservation hall of housing
that could be open
and he knows is not:

you must pay willingly
for this, for the future.

> *Can't you see*
> *what love and heartache's done to me*
> *I'm not the same as I used to be*
> *this is my last affair*

4

To his daughter, Rachel,
woman of perfect pitch
who does not perform
in public, or pose *live*,
he has bound this book
and had it signed,
first edition,
reminding her that Ralph & Fanny
sent her a check
when she was a freshwoman:

she should write her own *pass*.

In our actual state of affairs,
which is the currency of democracy
night and day / day and night
she will prepare
as Inman Page did
for the acts
of enabling
which was his
song.

He remembers patterns
in *Invisible Man:*
the chapters & verse of the sonata,
the cycle of the trine,
its structural schema
(all the paper talismans)
in the novel of becoming,
with boomerang, threnody
3   x   3   x   3
purpose / passion / perception
with seams of initiation:
scholarship / seven letters / dismissal
papers / brotherhood nameslip /
anonymous letter / sambo doll:
that which is taken: trained incapacity
that which is given: antagonistic cooperation
establishment to
antiestablishment
to self-recognition

ranter becomes writer

and he knows that on the artful frequencies
she speaks for him

SIX

~

Prologue of an Arkansas Traveler

"The Arkansas Traveler"
—A painting by Edward Payson Washburn
—An American strategy of humor in which Americans face their critics by pretending to be even dumber than they are expected to be, all the while undercutting their opponents by a play of witty double entendre. (The classic encounter is between a farmer and a city slicker, but a close look at the opposing values reveals that the antagonists symbolize the New World and the Old.)

Prologue of an Arkansas Traveler

"We rely on the truth for and against ourselves."
—Ralph Waldo Emerson, December 1847
"To the Public," *Massachusetts Quarterly Review*

Poppa Greer happened
Down Arkansaw way,
An' ast for a job
At Big Pete's Cafe.
—From "Slim Lands a Job?"
by Sterling A. Brown

Most men lied about New York City;
every woman tells the truth about trains.

I was scared of folks dipping snuff
and having to spit; old four eyes
lying about his age; I got about eight
notes from Chicago how to keep safe
on trains: one note is from Agnes
about nightwatchman, so I'm going
to ask Grandpa Brock
when I get to Hot Springs:

Grandpa's a ladies' man;
you can tell by his carriage,
a gait with a limp that keeps
his Stetson in place, bearing
like a man with a load
he's not about to drop,
dressed to kill,
polishing his own watch,
a timepiece worked from steelmills
until arthritis got him, moved:

sold his only house
in the hills above the Colorado
so his granddaughter,
Fanny Mae, could go to school:
she had done good time and bad
at the *Chicago Defender*—
you should read their secret
files on lynching,
with copies to the magnates
running these railroads:
grown men begging white men to change.

So I went to Fisk; getting there
was like the day Cesar Chavez
died; Hispanics rose up
in front of the Jubilee portrait
of the Fisk Singers
and began to testify about the fields:
the blacks in the audience were speechless
for a change. I thought of James Weldon's
wife not letting anybody, student
or no student, sit on her couch
with those crocheted cushions.

Professor Johnson wanted visitors,
students anxious to learn his craft,
but Miss Grace was in no mood
for visitors: I met her downtown
1946!

Said I should be ashamed of my company,
a writer, with a name like that, putting
you in the secretary block:
profane writers, irresponsible
for allowing me to work at day jobs
while basking in egotism, "writin' books."

What does that say about her husband:

IF YOU WANT TO GO TO MEMPHIS
YOU HAVE TO CHANGE TRAINS
AT EL DORADO:
                    so I'm writing to Grandpa
about folks spitting snuff juice
in paper bags my sandwiches were in.

I was seeing prisoners in a special car
chained to their residence;
as penance for their miserable condition
I gave candy to a poor woman
who had to change at Memphis:
of course the porter gave her advice—
the brakeman pointed out the scenery—
"pay particular attention to the swamp,"
he said.
                    Later I had come from Washington
to work in New York and I asked "Spinky"
to introduce me to a nice man,
with a brain for exercise, one
who could dance; I met "Waldo"
on home leave, we went to Frank's
where the dumplings were cheap
on a handwritten menu, beautiful hand, too.

"Waldo," as we shall call him,
had a thousand dollars in big bills
from the merchant marine:
he was sick of not fighting back
though not a Tuskegee Airman,
he went to study with William Dawson,
and fell into books,
taught how to ride trains by "Charlie,"
light enough to pass, and on a bridge
going around the state of Arkansas,
which all blacks had to avoid
or end up on that *Defender* secret
list: you remember those *white fence*
singers in "Don't You Want to Be Free"

put on by the *Negro People's Theatre:*
I wrote to Langston about that,
put on 7 days a week, between oxtail soup
encounters: we were always in the soup.

I'm thinking about Grandpa chained to those prisoners
in that special car: when I get to Hot Springs
I'm going to ask him about that shotgun
he put up against Jordan's face—
my mother's boyfriend, never saw Jordan
again: Grandpa's residence in '29
was I.O.U. Boathouse, a residence:
he was the nightclerk,
read everything, preparing for his grand-
daughter to see the work of traveling:
had arranged for a car
so she could see the sights:
Sites: poison ivy, not oak;
state flag, which was designed by a relative—
blue-bordered white diamond on a rectangular
field of red (for blood); 25 stars at the border.
Apple blossom, state flower; pine for lynching
tree; mockingbird for Wonder State
because of wide varieties in nature:
such as: spring livestock show in Pine Bluff—
they sing 11 A.M. convocation
"Lift Every Voice and Sing"
1100 strong at the black school—
tears in everybody's eyes—
I mean everybody! All those festivals
in and out of small towns:
tomato, grape, peach, cotton picking,
duck calling, bird-dog field trials,
greyhound racing, the Negro Leagues,
fox hunting and "Sister Goose":

Sister Goose was swimming on the lake;
she was arrested for swimming:
the sheriff was a fox, and the deputy

was a fox, the bailiff was a fox,
the jury was a fox (all foxes),
the judge, she was a fox:
and they gave Sister Goose a fair
trial, and found her guilty,
and prepared her, and ate her,
and they picked her bones clean.

So the state was beautiful, White River
particularly in the National Forest,
Little Missouri Falls in Ouachita;
Ozark Ike (that's cartoons), Mt. Magazine
and Sam's Throne—Delta Cottonfield,
Riverbend protection, St. Francis Levee,
water hyacinths, virgin stands of pine,
a swinging bridge—nofishingallowed!

I refused to be baptized, in the river,
because of public safety—you figure that out.

They got a traveling grocery store,
kin to the commissary,
full of seeds and dry bones.
You should see those wagons
near the general store.

Grandpa was a fiddler; he was never
a sharecropper, though on Sunday
he loves to be in their company:

Stay off the Rice-Fix Show Boat,
you hear me—he would laugh—
that's not a car ferry, nor is it freight:

try to study architecture at Fisk:
good residence, to draw, are more than able
on Pulaski Heights, or the outskirts
of El Dorado, Elizabethan half-timbered,
nearby Norman adaptation,
near that modified Georgian,
a few doors down, International Style,
at least one wall of glass brick,

long lines, flat roof, a world
of play on the horizontal:
always live on the vertical,
dream on the horizontal:

teaches you about your dwellings:

don't throw away those Indian names

don't forget how they were cajoled
and/or conquered: study who and why
folks wanted to change, or keep,
the name Arkansas—look up the origins
of the dice box; find out if C. T. Davis
is worth reading, poet laureate, I hear.

Don't skip juvenile books; find out
what is news to journalists, why their memoirs,
what left to grazing, what fallow, what singed.

Study the "Toby Shows": this is a history
of America in a nutshell; I already told
you about the music industry in this state.

The play, as put on in N.Y.C., was too full
of pistol shots, bowie knives, bad-playing
fiddlers: somebody dreamed this all up
in the St. Charles Hotel in New Orleans:

always search out the theft; some collectors,
academics, and friends of our people, cry
over hymnals: beware of hymnals.

When they tell you "Negroes" don't have song-
books; they think we have refrain in the genes:
remember, these songs were converted
into union songs—they say these tunes
came from Harlem: when the crew grunts
watch out for radio, what year did the work-
gangs complete the Memphis & Little Rock Railroad?
1871: how many thousands gone during folksay
reconstruction / resurrection / lynching bee: those tunes!

Study the lifelines of Catlin's full-length Indians;
they say that handicraft was never commercialized
in Arkansas; study Washburn's painting of our namesake;
his daddy was a missionary sent to the Arkansas Cherokee;
oils of Byrd stock the state capitol gallery, mules
of the confederacy: Lee, Jeff Davis, Stonewall, the Klan.

Many of the pioneers arrived in flatboats: Wolf Cabin,
postmaster art from the F.W.A. called clearing the land,
the confederate capitol in Little Rock, Henderliter House;
original canvas of *Arkansas Traveler,* nothing of the copyright;
Judge Isaac Parker's "men who rode for Parker" us deputy
     marshals
attached to the court: mucho shotguns, mucho mustaches/hats.

Did you know they washed for diamonds, even newsmen and
     their wives
in 1910: at this time 4000 Negroes live in El Dorado;
they find little work in the oil fields, more as domestics:
theymightfindworkinthecoalminesofSebastianCounty:

trapezoids and triangle additions confuse local traffic,
but there are oaks for lynch, excuse my obsession,
elms, maple, poplars: study the nature and genus of trees
to study the DNA of black blood as the sap / taproot /
     underground
architecture of root canals, bridgework, cleft palates
needing reconstructive surgery, volunteer work, horseracing
stock, exchange:
                         now about hot springs: first white men
probably De Soto; braves from competing tribes gather,
compress hot mud to their aching trail bruises, in harmony:
of course, legendary, as prehistorically guesswork:
let me tell you about steel, blast furnaces, I would talk
to the Natchitoches Indians if I were you, and quoting from
the text of their legends: The water has a charge of carbonic
acid, lime taste, tufa deposits, moss encrustations not
     putrefactions
by healing for the industry of cotton at the gin, press, oil
refinery, loading log train, sawmill, papermill, bauxite plant,

quicksilver reduction furnace, corncob pipe factory, carpenter
    dam;
that's enough, child. I forgot points of interest:

1. Army/Navy General Hospital
    2. Hot Springs National Park Administration Building
        3. Quapaw Bathhouse
4. Fordyce Bathhouse (electric hoist for paralytics)
                    5. Display Hot Spring
6. Arlington Park (weeping willow—will weep for me): tufa,
    porous rock
with silica/calcite salt deposits, encrustations, covered with
moss, 15' thick 7. Hot Springs National Park (more than a
1000 acres), picnicking fools paradise for days there. 8. Old
Catholic School (private), after 1922, became rooming house;
have stayed there. 9. Whittington Park (spring training center
for major leagues before Jackie) 10. Leo N. Levi Memorial
Hospital (supported by Jewish groups and individuals; pay
attention to entryway: huge magnolia, twins, spreading four
stories high—no lynchings reported so far in black press—
I'm sorry, honey)

                    11. Oaklawn
Jockey Club (please understand pari-mutuel betting; give and
    take on whether
gambling, horseracing was legal, or not; lots of confusion on
    that score:
many jockeys passing for white; stopover for many stables in
    South-North
circuit. Roosevelt investigated this Arkansas Derby secretly:
    no results!

Look at the brows of plantation hands,
even the ones on horseback, and watch
their hands; wagonloads of cotton at the gin
Lehi, please synchronize philanthropy with industrial
base hit; Fedora is Ferda Plantation at Plum Bayou
in the speech pattern of a stuttering boy: black or white.

Ozark couples are plain, and plainspoken: the cutsaw
for large trees in the hills is a fine-toothed comb:

they have a ritual for haystacks, corn in shocks,
herding mules, sheep grazing, no hanky-panky with them mules
and watch those mules eat sorghum, which is cane-work
no white man is bound to respect, or do,
but threshing rice is combining, almost, raking
soybean hay is a larkspur afternoon,
in the evening, judging cattle at show,
judging at stockyards.

I have heard great black singing at the War Memorial
Building in Little Rock, 1911, before troops came
home, and I have blessed those children ambling next
to troops ambivalent in their purpose: State Line Avenue
in Texarkana produced the best con-woman in the world:
Willie Mae, who introduced her daughter to Abbey Lincoln
in Bakersfield—this was long before NOTHING BUT A MAN.
Willie Mae was so quick and so sweet she went to Beverly
Hills, exclusive clientele only, si vous plait, and heisted the food
money from the investors in Orange County oranges
even before *Chinatown;* Willie Mae visited her mother
at the border of these two evil states and still transcribed
sacred songs invented in the canebrakes, and washed in the A.
River, worked at Bathhouse Row, Eureka Springs, Tibbetts
House in Fayetteville, Simmons House, Pine Bluff,
contributed to the Fine Arts Building in Little Rock,
and never attended any functions that had her name on it.

She was caught in the Lakeview Resettlement Community, black,
and recitation, lake dick resettlement community school,
was seen making her own school lunch program, integrated,
and was caught on camera feeding cod-liver oil in the nursery
school at Lakeview; she handed out cod-liver samples on public
health nurse visits: didn't discriminate at Parnell Hall
for the deaf, knew farmboys, log cabin rehab station
dormitory at Jonesboro, arm wrestled with Gov. Bill Murray
and whipped his elbow into a chickenwishbonefriggazi.

(Inoculated at swimming holes, fed wild ducks, hunted quail,
ate quail, fished in cane pole reverie singing about her mother,

who had just passed; understood paddock at the track,
    equestriennes
under magnolias were no deep river to her; fished in Lake
    Wanona;
boycotted the state fishery, state hatchery, Lonoke: knew her state
chronology: De Soto; "Mississippi Bubble" bursts; Spain returns
Louisiana to France by secret treaty; District of Arkansas
set up as partial payment for Louisiana Purchase; Quapaw Treaty
and ceding of lands between rivers, Arkansas and Red; Cherokee
agree to leave Arkansas; Sam Houston's revolution plan; Federal
    troops
burn Napoleon (look that up!); Poll tax; Convict Leasing Law;
Elaine race riot; state-owned bridges made toll free: quilt that!

Notes

From the *OED*

HONOURABLE, HONORABLE: A. *adj.* 1. Worthy of being honoured; entitled to honour, respect, esteem, or reverence. a. Of persons. b. Of things. c. Respectable in quality or amount; considerable; decent. 2. a. Holding a position of honour; of distinguished rank; noble; illustrious. b. Applied as an official or courtesy title of honour or distinction. 3. a. Of things: Characterized by or accompanied with honour; bringing or fraught with honour to the possessor. *honourable mention* b. Consistent with honour or reputation. 4. Showing or doing honour; honouring. 5. Characterized by principles of honour, probity, or rectitude; upright, honest: the reverse of base. a. Of persons. b. Of things. B. *sb.* a. An honourable or distinguished person. b. One who has the title of Honourable. So *Right Honourable.* (colloq.) C. *adv.* Honourably.

AMENDMENT: The action of amending, whether in process, or as completed. 1. Removal of faults, correction, reformation. a. Of human conduct. *absol.* = self-reformation. b. Of faults or errors in things, as a book, a law, etc. c. *Law.* Correction of error in a write or process. d. The alteration of a bill before Parliament. Hence *concr.* A clause, paragraph, or words proposed to be substituted for others, or to be inserted, in a bill (the result of the adoption of which may even be to defeat the measure; see AMEND 4). e. *In a public meeting.* A proposed alteration in the terms of a resolution submitted to a meeting for adoption; *extended to* a resolution proposed instead of or in opposition to another; a countermotion. 2. Repair, mending (of things damaged). *Obs.* 3. General "improvement" of condition. 4. Improvement in health, recovery from illness. 5. Amends-making, reparation. *Obs.* 6. "Improvement" of the soil; *concr.* that which improved the soil, manure. *Obs.*

"Ulysses S. Grant: His Prose"—The poem is imagined as a dialogue with Mark Twain at Mt. McGregor, where Grant was finishing his memoirs to support his family. Clemons was instrumental in seeing this "literary exercise" to completion.

"To an Old Man Twiddlin' Thumbs" refers to the poet Sterling Allen Brown. The last line echoes Brown's anthem "Strong Men."

"Songlines from a Tessera(e) Journal" is in memory of the life and times of the painter and collagist Romare Bearden.

"Archives" ends with a proverbial affirmation assigned to Ernie Banks, the Chicago Cub Hall of Famer; it is also a code for the attitude of all ballplayers connected with the Negro Leagues, a call for all-comers. The poem is written for the poet's son, Patrice Cuchulain Harper, fifteen and a high school baseball and football player in Hamilton, N.Y.

The subject of "Jest: A Collection of Records" is Bob Blackmore, professor emeritus at Colgate University. For many years he hosted a jazz program on local radio in Hamilton, N.Y. He is an expert gardener, collector of Americana, and a raconteur on first editions, ensembles large and small, and race records.

"Hinton's Silkscreens" refers to the life and career of the painter Alfred Fontaine Hinton, who teaches at the University of Michigan, Ann Arbor.

The dedicatees of the poem "The Beauty Shell" are mother and son.

The repair session cited in "Fixit" is also a dialogue overheard of how insiders relate to one another. "Lady Flip" is Flip Phillips, excellent journeyman of his instrument. Phillips was ever-respectful of genius; the innovator and "President" Lester Young was his model for an entire generation. Young gave poetic monikers to friends and foes alike and called Billie Holiday "Lady Day"; she called him "the President." Pres called his instrument "My People." Young was a prime maker, his own category.

"Dexter Leaps In" is in memory of Dexter Gordon, the tenor saxophonist. The epigraph is from the movie *'Round Midnight,* featuring Gordon as hero.

" 'Dixie Peach' " recalls the early life of Langston Hughes in Lawrence, Kansas. Nicodemus was a planned all-black community. Dixie Peach is a hair pomade.

"Saint Sassy Divine" is the praisesong for the singer Sarah Vaughan.

"Teaching Institutes" was written for Harriet Waltzer Sheridan and read to introduce the Sheridan Memorial Lecture Series at Brown University on April 6, 1994.

"Mr. Knowlton Predicts" refers to Daniel Knowlton, university bookbinder in the John Hay and Rockefeller Libraries at Brown University for four decades. He is a master of book design.

In "Madam Tutu," the characters of "Mule" and "Madam Tutu" are son and mother, respectively.

"The Ghost of Soul-making" is a trope from the poet John Keats. Ruth Oppenheim is a survivor of Kristallnacht, which she witnessed as a child.

"Advice to Clinton" has an epigraph from Lincoln's second inaugural address. "Immigration parade" refers to Haiti; the "Arkansas Traveler" is a character from American folklore, a song, a folktale from Black American folksay, and a quilt with a distinct, cutaway geometric pattern.

Dorothy Parker left her estate to Martin Luther King Jr. The incident of failed speech cited in "Protégé: 1962" occurred in a course she taught on popular literature at the poet's alma mater, in Los Angeles. She died in 1967.

"The Revolutionary Garden" was written for the inauguration of Brown University's president Vartan Gregorian.

"Thimble" refers to Henrietta, the first black undertaker in the United States, a resident of Philadelphia, and a conductor on the underground railroad; she was the maternal ancestor of the poet's mother.

"Parenting" alludes to commencement weekend 1983 at Brown University, when the poet was honored as the first occupant of the Israel J. Kapstein Professor of English chair and introduced at the ceremony by Kappy, the venerable writer, teacher, and master of Coleridge. The refrain is from "Last Affair: Bessie's Blues Song," by the poet. Part 4 of the poem refers to the poet's daughter, Rachel, who was graduated from Brown in 1994. Fanny and Ralph are Mr. and Mrs. Ralph Ellison. Brown University held a festival in honor of Mr. Ellison upon his retirement from teaching in 1979.

The second epigraph to "Prologue of an Arkansas Traveler" is taken from Sterling A. Brown's *Collected Poems,* selected by the poet for the National Poetry Series in 1980.

Illinois Poetry Series
Laurence Lieberman, Editor

Collected Poems, 1930–83
Josephine Miles (1983)

The River Painter
Emily Grosholz (1984)

Healing Song for the Inner Ear
Michael S. Harper (1984)

The Passion of the Right-Angled
Man
T. R. Hummer (1984)

Dear John, Dear Coltrane
Michael S. Harper (1985)

Poems from the Sangamon
John Knoepfle (1985)

In It
Stephen Berg (1986)

The Ghosts of Who We Were
Phyllis Thompson (1986)

Moon in a Mason Jar
Robert Wrigley (1986)

Lower-Class Heresy
T. R. Hummer (1987)

Poems: New and Selected
Frederick Morgan (1987)

Furnace Harbor: A Rhapsody of
the North Country
Philip D. Church (1988)

Bad Girl, with Hawk
Nance Van Winckel (1988)

Blue Tango
Michael Van Walleghen (1989)

Eden
Dennis Schmitz (1989)

Waiting for Poppa at the
Smithtown Diner
Peter Serchuk (1990)

Great Blue
Brendan Galvin (1990)

What My Father Believed
Robert Wrigley (1991)

Something Grazes Our Hair
S. J. Marks (1991)

Walking the Blind Dog
G. E. Murray (1992)

The Sawdust War
Jim Barnes (1992)

The God of Indeterminacy
Sandra McPherson (1993)

Off-Season at the Edge of the
World
Debora Greger (1994)

Counting the Black Angels
Len Roberts (1994)

Oblivion
Stephen Berg (1995)

To Us, All Flowers Are Roses
Lorna Goodison (1995)

Honorable Amendments
Michael S. Harper (1995)

Points of Departure
Miller Williams (1995)

National Poetry Series

Eroding Witness
Nathaniel Mackey (1985)
Selected by Michael S. Harper

Palladium
Alice Fulton (1986)
Selected by Mark Strand

Cities in Motion
Sylvia Moss (1987)
Selected by Derek Walcott

The Hand of God and a Few
Bright Flowers
William Olsen (1988)
Selected by David Wagoner

The Great Bird of Love
Paul Zimmer (1989)
Selected by William Stafford

Stubborn
Roland Flint (1990)
Selected by Dave Smith

The Surface
Laura Mullen (1991)
Selected by C. K. Williams

The Dig
Lynn Emanuel (1992)
Selected by Gerald Stern

My Alexandria
Mark Doty (1993)
Selected by Philip Levine

The High Road to Taos
Martin Edmunds (1994)
Selected by Donald Hall

Theater of Animals
Samn Stockwell (1995)
Selected by Louise Glück

Other Poetry Volumes

Local Men and *Domains*
James Whitehead (1987)

Her Soul beneath the Bone:
Women's Poetry on Breast Cancer
Edited by Leatrice Lifshitz (1988)

Days from a Dream Almanac
Dennis Tedlock (1990)

Working Classics: Poems on
Industrial Life
*Edited by Peter Oresick and Nicholas
Coles* (1990)

Hummers, Knucklers, and Slow
Curves: Contemporary Baseball
Poems
Edited by Don Johnson (1991)

The Double Reckoning of
Christopher Columbus
Barbara Helfgott Hyett (1992)

Selected Poems
Jean Garrigue (1992)

New and Selected Poems, 1962–92
Laurence Lieberman (1993)

The Dig and *Hotel Fiesta*
Lynn Emanuel (1994)

For a Living: The Poetry of Work
*Edited by Nicholas Coles and Peter
Oresick* (1995)